ISTANBUL - 2014

The author	: **Osman Nuri TOPBAŞ**
Copy editor	: **Gabriel Fouad HADDAD**
Translator	: **Selman CUL**
Redactor	: **Hikmet YAMAN**
Graphics	: **Rasim SHAKIROV**
ISBN	: **978-9944-83-099-7**

WORLD GRAPHICS

Adres: Bulgurlu Mah. Çiçek Sok. No:35
Küçük Çamlıca, Üsküdar, İstanbul / Türkiye
info@islamicpublishing.net - www.islamicpublishing.net
Tel: (+90 216) 428 49 36 Fax: (+90 216) 428 49 36

The Secret in the Love for God

Contents

About the author 5
Preface 7
The secret in the love of Allah 10
The Perfect Man 20
Standing firm on the path of Allah 31
Being with the righteous and the truthful 40
Sincerity towards Allah 49
Fear and Hope 60
Heedlessness 71
The beautification of death 81
Rizq (sustenance) 92
Light and Darkness 105
Excellence (Ihsān) and Vigilance (Murāqabah) 115
Mankind's Reality 127
Selflessness (īthār) 133
Islam Gives Life to Mankind 143
The Significance of Manners in Tasawwuf 156
Love (mahabbah) 167
Interview of Osman Nuri Topbaş on tasawwuf 182

About the author

Osman Nuri Topbaş was born in 1942 in Erenkoy, Istanbul, Turkey to Musa Topbaş and Fatma Feride Hanim, H. Fahri Kigili's daughter. He went to Erenkoy Zihni Pasa Primary School and, in 1953, Istanbul Imam Hatip High School, one of the leading secondary educational institutions with highly respected teachers such as M. Celaleddin Ökten, Mahir İz, and Nureddin Topçu. During that time, he studied under the supervision of M. Zekai Konrapa, Yaman Dede (Abdülkadir Keçeoğlu), Ahmet Davutoğlu, Mahmud Bayram, and Ali Rızâ Sağman. He also became acquainted with famous poet and thinker Necip Fazil. He joined the latter's circle of friends, attended his speeches, followed his magazine *Büyük Doğu*, and became an ardent supporter of his ideas. Both Osman and his uncle Abidin Topbaş graduated from high school in 1960.

After graduation, Topbaş engaged in trade and industry for some time. In 1962 he performed his military service in Tillo, Siirt as a reserve officer teacher. He loved teaching and being involved with people when he was in the army.

Having completed military service, Topbaş went back to trade but he never severed himself from learning and philanthropy. He was an active member of Ilim Yayma Cemiyeti (Association for the Promulgation of Knowledge). His business site operated like a charitable organization and foundation; it was a center for giving scholarships to students and assistance to the poor. He was also in charge of his family's philanthropic services. He continued his charitable activities under the roof of Hüdâyi endowment after its foundation in 1985. He was instrumental not only in its foundation but also in spreading its services to students from neighboring countries.

Topbaş began to write in the early 1990s as a result of his interest in religious studies and poetry. Among his works published in Istanbul:

1. *Bir Testi Su* (1996), translated into English as *Tears of the Heart*.

2. *Rahmet Esintileri* (1997), translated to English as *Prophet of Mercy*.

3. *Nebiler Silsilesi I- IV* (1997-1998).

4. *Tarihten Günümüze İbret Işıkları* (1998).

5. *Abide Şahsiyetleri ve Müessesleriyle Osmanlı* (1999).

6. *İslam İman İbadet* (2000), translated into English as *Islam: Spirit and Form*.

7. *Muhabbetteki Sır* (2001). The present book is its translation from Turkish to English based on the 2001 edition.

8. *İmandan İhsana Tasavvuf* (2002).

9. *Vakıf-İnfak-Hizmet* (2002).

10. *Son Nefes* (2003).

Topbaş's books have been translated into several languages. He has shared his vision also through teaching seminars, speaking at conferences and chairing panels in many different countries.

He is married and has four children.

Preface

Praise be to Allah the Exalted who has blessed us, His powerless servants, with the joy and peace of true faith. Blessings and peace be upon the Endless Pride of the universe, Prophet Muhammad, who has led humanity from darkness to boundless light.

Allah Almighty has bestowed upon existence a unique secret: He has created it out of love. Because of this, there is decline wherever love does not exist and there are manifestations of perfection wherever it exists. As Rumi's *Mathnawi* explains it:

Allah whispered a secret into the ear of a cloud, and tears of water poured down from its eyes like a bucket. He whispered a secret into the ear of a rose and beautified it with colours and fragrance. He whispered a secret to a stone and turned it into shimmering carnelian in the mine. He bestowed a secret to a human being and exalted the ones who protected it to eternity.

That secret is the secret of love. That is why the only way for a human being to reach Allah Almighty's good pleasure and the intercession of the Prophet (upon him blessings and peace) – and consequently gain salvation in this world and the hereafter – is a simple truth hidden inside the secret of love. Those know this truth and are obedient to its precepts experience intense emotion and exhilaration in their hearts just like the crying tree stump which cried out of love for the Prophet (upon him blessings and peace). For living at such a level of love exalts a human being to a state of perfection and the zenith of creation. It leads to the straight path.

However, to stay on the straight path is only possible through the company of the righteous and truthful believers. Such fellowship builds up the balance of soul and body until the sultan-soul prevails over the slave-body. The heart – the place where the divine manifestations appear – achieves tranquility and relief because it can reach the Truth.

The servant progresses on the way to spiritual perfection, facing various trials of faith. At every stage of this journey to eternity, he or she is treated in proportion to his or her sincerity. The key to Allah's mercy and grace lies in one's straddling fear and hope – a very important munition to win the war against ambition and jealousy, and achieve contentment. A servant who has achieved this state will stay alert against the danger of heedlessness and worship his or her Lord with an alert and sound heart. By watching one's lower self, one strengthens one's heart toward controlling one's anger.

Thus those who can "be the real wrestlers" as in the saying of the Prophet (upon him blessings and peace)[1] comprehend the divine wisdom behind life and death. They do not put stock in the temporary pleasures of this world. They only try to do good deeds and live a life adorned with knowledge, understanding, servitude and worship. Because such a life would fill the heart with love of Truth, the servant realizes the serenity and beauty of death. He or she regards death as a reunion with the Beloved and eagerly waits for it.

---

1. Narrated by al-Bukhari and Muslim in their Sahihs.

Preface

A believer works to earn his licit sustenance in the day and gets spiritual nourishment through his or her prayers in the middle of the night. That is why they are neither concerned with the pursuit of sustenance nor tossed about with worldly anxiety. Their souls are like clouds spreading mercy around them. They become springs of serenity and blessings for their community, and their family turns into a paradise in this world.

In this world of trials where light and darkness fight mercilessly, those who are raised in that paradise always take the side of right and truth – the straight path shown by the divine commands. They rapturously perform their obligations towards the Holy Qur'an. They also try to read the silent and wordless book of the universe and find out its wisdom, mysteries and truths. Thus they turn into mirrors reflecting the spiritual prosperity and serenity bestowed upon them. This eminent state is the state of being a living Qur'an. Indeed all the righteous struggles, from the battle of Badr to the battles fought by our Ottoman ancestors, are efforts to reach and protect that eminent state.

This, then, is a summary of this humble book, which I have named *"From the Garden of the Heart: The Secret in the Love for Allah."*

May our Lord bestow upon us manifestations of prosperity and spirituality. May Allah grant us the ecstasy of faith. May He illuminate our hearts with the light of the Qur'an and draw out springs of wisdom in our perception. May our Lord grace us with His love, mercy and compassion.

Amin!

1.

The secret in the love of Allah

One of the most prominent attributes of the hidden treasure mentioned in the saying *"I was a secret treasure. I wanted to be known and so I created creation"* is absolute grace. Allah Almighty did not desire this mysterious, infinite and imperceptible grace to be concealed, so He created creation.

A small drop of His infinite love was granted to this universe and to this earth. Thus, the earth gained superiority over other creations; Allah also created the human being, the most honorable creature, from the earth.

Allah, who created all creatures with love, made them a sign of His artistry and perfection. The existence of the human being as a divine masterpiece has become the perfect manifestation of love and kindness. For the purpose of this world's creation was not solely to adorn it with green fields, valleys, vast deserts and mountains; it was the human being – the spring of love and the quintessence of creation. For that reason, the honor of a human being is in direct proportion his preserving this objective of his own creation.

Furthermore, since the reason for creation is love, the attribute of love is present as a natural inclination in all creatures. Even a scorpion's conveyance of its offspring on its back is the result of this love.

The secret in the love of Allah

This inclination of love is at its peak in a human being, the most honorable of creatures. Nevertheless, in this world filled with trials and tribulations, man will obtain the reward of his love to the extent of the worthiness of his beloved. This means that the human heart, created with the ability of infinite love, can only reach perfection if its possessor directs his tendency towards love of Allah. He cannot help himself by pursuing inferior and useless goals – ultimately life would end in disappointment. In other words, only as long as man devotes to Allah and those beloved to Him his natural tendency to love, can he acquire the blessing to ascend spiritually to the extent of his devotion.

Indeed, divine tests inflicted upon a human being depend upon how he directs his love. It is because of this rule that Allah granted human nature negative inclinations as well as positive ones. Allah has granted human beings a share of his three great attributes: 1) absolute existence, 2) absolute grace and 3) absolute good; but He has also impaired him with the opposites of these attributes: 1) absolute non-existence, 2) absolute ugliness and 3) absolute evil. In this context, the Qur'an says: "And He inspired it (the soul) [with conscience of] what is wrong for it and what is right for it." (*Shams*, 91:8)

These are the two infinite, diametrically opposite poles to which human beings are attracted throughout their lives. It must be realized that the greatest misfortune of man is his inclination towards the negative pole. Those who are inclined to this pole are so blinded that they only admire themselves and their actions. This is a big weakness. Such heedlessness that prevents the human being from realising his or her full potential. It is also the most harmful spiritual illness and great arrogance for a human being who then becomes a foreigner to divine power.

The Secret in the Love for God

The real meaning in the Sufi saying *"Die before death comes to you!"* is that one should avoid falling into the trap of acquiring the bad traits which stem from the negative pole and should, instead, escape from the whirlpool of nature. However, the method for such realization does not mean to kill the self *(nafs)* but to gain control over it. Rūmī explains this point as follows:

> *If the water remains underneath the ship, it becomes a point of support. However, if it fills the ship it will destroy it. One can exemplify the same fact with the fire moving the ship. The fire in the boiler moves the ship. But if this fire spreads into the deck then it will burn the ship.*

A servant therefore becomes close to his Lord inasmuch as he stems the effects of negative traits. The only way to achieve this is to steer one's love towards Allah to the extent of the capacity of one's heart. Yet many dangers lurk in directly steering one's love towards Allah. At one point the heart may burn as if electrified with high voltage. This may destroy a person. The manifestation of Allah to the Prophet Moses (upon him blessings and peace) is a good example of this.

Moses (upon him blessings and peace) encountered the *Kalām* or speech attribute of Allah on Mount Sinai. He lost his consciousness to great love because of the spiritual attractiveness of divine conversation beyond the perception of a human being – without letters or words. Then he fervently asked to see Allah. But Allah replied, "You cannot see me!" When he insisted, Allah told him to glance at the mountain: the mountain was shattered by a shaft of light sent from Allah. After this terrifying event, Moses (upon him blessings and peace) fainted and asked for Allah's forgiveness.

The secret in the love of Allah

As this incident shows, love requires gradation. Certain practices are needed in order to develop one's ability to experience divine love. This requires gradual training through embracing the spirituality of Allah's friends and moving away from the authority of self. The heart can only increase its inborn ability to love by this kind of training, and can thus be purified and freed from the grip of negative traits. Only then can it gain the spiritual capacity to become a reflector of divine love, like a polished mirror.

The love of mother, father, wife, husband and children, and material and spiritual opportunities and other worldly favors are all Allah's kindness and favor to His servants. But all these kinds of love should be a means to reach Allah. They are only signposts in Allah's path. Our hearts should not be slaves to them, for those who are in love with Absolute Beauty do not fall in love with fragments. Those who do will be deprived of the whole. In other words, those who fall in love with the world will be deprived of Allah's love. Rūmī expresses this in the following couplet:

Those who fall in love with the world are like hunters who shoot at shadows;
how could a shadow come into their possession?
One of the foolish people tried to catch a bird's shadow;
but even the bird on the branch was bewildered about this.

Every conscious person who thinks of his or her end can easily understand that it is the purpose of creation that one has to limit their indulgence in amusements and temporary affection by directing his or her love towards Allah. Absolute grace is the grace of Allah. All of the beauties we witness with admiration are nothing but a reflection of His beauty.

The love between Leylā and Majnūn is a magnificent example of this fact. If Majnūn's heart had remained devoted to Leyla, she would have become his idol. However, Leylā only played a temporary role for Majnūn and she fell from his favor after elevating his heart to a level where its object became divine love. Although Majnūn had set off on his journey toward Leylā, he showed the power to steer his heart towards Allah, not settle upon Leylā.

Love is accepted only as long as its aim is true. Such kind of love does not become a mansion, absolute headquarter, and final destination for the heart if it ends up with delusion and disappointment! Only free from such may the heart continue its journey with the blessings acquired from these loves like a fertile soil. The danger here lies in turning towards those who are not fit to be loved. Worse yet is to remain stuck on them. If Majnūn had been smothered with his infatuation with Leylā without moving past her, his love would have been worthless. He would have disappeared with finite love just like so many other Majnūns.

Allah Almighty did not abandon the prophet Joseph (upon him blessings and peace) who bore in himself the light of Prophethood when he was thrown into a well by his brothers. A thirsty traveller lowered a bucket into the well supposing that there would be some water below. When Joseph (upon him blessings and peace) came out with the bucket, the perceptive traveller forgot his thirst. He was charmed and terrified with the beauty he beheld. The heedless traveller, on the other hand, did not see the spiritual aspect of this beauty. He remained focussed on the material substance, which he unwarily sold at a cheap price – just like the Majnūn who remained stuck on Leylā and could not eventually achieve divine union.

For the traveller who lowered the rope into the well in the hope of finding water, it should have been a great opportunity to forget the water when he saw Joseph's (upon him blessings and peace) beauty. He should have severed all his finite and relative dealings before the manifestation of divine love which shone like the sun's bright rays through a lens. It was a great pity that the foolish traveller was duped by the lure of worldly advantages he calculated he would receive through Joseph (upon him blessings and peace). He thus wasted the golden opportunity that was presented to him.

What we are trying to explain here is the ideal course to realise the greatest love and most lasting affection. Passing through stages of love without getting stuck is beyond the capacity of most ordinary people. Those who reach perfection are those who incline towards this goal externally by the choice of their free will and internally by the drive of their destiny. These people can reach variously advanced stages through many paths, all of them guiding to Allah in proportion to the divine aid they are granted. The outcome is the return to Allah – *fanā' fī Allāh* (annihilation in Allah) – like the river's disappearance into the sea. The ultimate destination is *baqā' bi-Allāh* (abiding with Allah).[2]

One should know that the limit of reason is finite. Anything beyond the limit of reason is madness. However, the capacity of the heart is infinite. The point of tranquillity is annihilation in Allah and eternity with Allah. Rūmī beautifully expresses how he was burned with divine love in a state of *fanā' fī Allāh* and *baqā' bi-Allāh* and how this fire within his soul would not be extinguished even by death:

---

2. *Fanā' fī Allāh* as a concept in *tasawwuf* means the permanent eradication in the heart of all qualities that are disliked by Allah (*al-akhlāq al-dhamīmah*). It requires complete elimination of desires emanating from the *nafs*. It is also called *takhliyah*, which means "emptying" the heart forever from what is not supposed to be there. The concept of *Baqā' bi Allāh* as used in *tasawwuf* denotes permanently internalising in the heart the good qualities that are loved by Allah. It is the result of complete and continuous submission to the will of Allah. It is also called *tahliyah*, which means the "ornamentation" or "beautification" of the heart in an enduring manner with good qualities (*al-akhlāq al-hamīdah*) that are permanently rooted there.

Open my grave after my death and see how fumes will rise from my shroud! What makes death frightening is this bodily cage. When you break the shell of the body you will see that death will look like pearls!

One of the most important attributes of the friends of Allah is to be consumed by divine love. Rūmī searched for the real lovers who were burned in love, hence those impassioned expressions. He states this desire as follows:

I need such a lover that from his inner flames great tumults should take place; and with the fire of his heart even fires should become ashes.

There are two kinds of love: real and metaphorical.

Love, addiction and devotion to any being in the universe "other than Allah" (*mā siwā Allāh*) are a metaphorical love, whereas love for Lord of the universe and inclination towards Him is real love.

Those who have polished their hearts with the real love for the Lord can see how beauty is reflected in themselves at all times and witness one of Allah's unlimited signs of power. In other words, they discover within their nature the reality of *ahsani taqwīm* (the most excellent pattern). For them, there are no metaphorical colors and odors attracting us with their beauty but something exceedingly truer. For they have reached to the knowledge of Allah. They have given up external adornments and reached to Reality. There, they beheld divine eternity.

The great curtain drawn between Allah and His servants is not a physical distance like earth and sky. This curtain is the feeling of a separate existence from the Creator. Because of this, Allah states "when I inspired into him a spirit from Me" and reminds human beings of the essence he had given from His presence. It was also said of Allah: "I am the secret of the human being, and the human being is the secret of Me."

Hence, the divine treasures and secrets are dedicated to humankind. Allah, the Almighty, wishes to present His sublime existence in the sacred frame of the human being. "I am the secret of man" contains the glad tidings of a shared attribute. If this essence and glad tidings canconvey a believer to the perfection of love and affection, then the heart begins to travel towards the secrets of the divine world. Thus, the reality of all objects, the secrets called "human" and "universe" and the secrets of the divine world may all appear. At that time the servant receives the manifestations of a sound heart.

When the servant has attained this maturity, the curtain of heedlessness between the servant and Allah is lifted little by little. The servant can understand the secret of "Die before you die." The world and its finite love, its temporary and transient beauty scatter into the wind. The soul perceives the great pleasure of approaching its Creator.

One should know that the only spring of mercy and affection to carry one to the ocean of Allah's love is the Prophet (upon him blessings and peace). Love of Muhammad (upon him blessings and peace) means love of Allah Most High. Obedience to him means obedience to Allah, and to rebel against him means to rebel against Allah. Therefore, the honorable existence of the Prophet Muhammad constitutes a place of love and refuge for mankind. The knowers ('ārifun) know that the reason for the existence of the creation is the love of Muhammad. Hence the entire universe is dedicated to the light of Muhammad's (upon him blessings and peace) existence.

It is for this reason that the love for the messenger of Allah (upon him blessings and peace) is protected from the dangers that lurk in the love for other beings (mā siwā). Accordingly, it is imperative to love the Prophet (upon him blessings and peace) wholeheartedly. Fātima (may Allah be pleased with her) presents one of the best examples of this love in her description of her state of despair at the Prophet's (upon him blessings and peace) funeral:

> *With the Prophet's honoring of the next world, such a calamity has come over me that, had it come over darkness, its color would have been changed. (Ibn al-Jawzi, al-Wafa.)*

The most beautiful and meaningful manifestation of love for the Prophet (upon him blessings and peace) appears in obedience to him. The principle of "The lover should love everything loved by his beloved" means it is actually necessary to obey the Prophet (upon him blessings and peace). This love constitutes the backbone of love for Allah. Any other love has been invalidated in the path of Quran and Sunnah. The only way to reach to divine love is through love of the Prophet Muhammad.

Love for the Prophet (upon him blessings and peace) is the highest state that a human could ever reach in the path of the love for Allah. Allah has placed limits on all human abilities including their perception and intelligence. However, His divine essence surpasses all limits.

Love for Allah requires love for Muhammad's light (*Nūr Muhammadī*), for his honorable existence, for the friends of Allah, and then for every creature esteemed in the presence of Allah to the extent of their merit. A circle of love in inclination towards Allah is a spring of mercy and recovery for souls. Any love outside this circle weakens the logic prevalent in love. Accordingly, there are huge blessings in love for the Prophet (upon him blessings and peace) and the people of Allah (*Ahl Allāh*). Remorse both in this world and the hereafter awaits those who hate them.

The secret in the love of Allah

The hearts of the friends of Allah are like mother-of-pearl. They beget pearls larger than raindrops in April. They can turn immature hearts into big pearls with the help of Allah. All that is needed for a seeker is to perceive the raindrop hidden in this pearl! In the commentary of the *Mathnawī* it is stated:

> Allah whispered a secret into the ear of a cloud, and tears of water poured down from its eyes like a bucket. He whispered a secret into the ear of a rose, and beautified it with colours and fragrance. He whispered a secret to a stone, and turned it into shimmering carnelian in the mine. With His graciousness He poured water from the cloud, beautified the rose and gave value to the stone.
>
> He whispered a secret to the human body and elevated to eternity those who kept this secret. Receiving inspiration from the divine world, these bodies attained the secret of closeness to Allah – being rescued from body.

Throughout history, prophets and messengers, who received this secret, have been the bearers of light who reached perfection through their love.

May Allah grant us the great favor of His affection, the affection of his beloved Prophet and his saints! May Allah not take back our lives until we have performed enough good deeds to ensure our acquittal in the next world and before he enlightened our hearts with magnificent manifestations of His love!

May Allah fill our hearts with mercy!

Amin!

2.
The Perfect Man

Man was created by Allah in the best way (*ahsani taqwīm*) and as such Man is the essence of all being. He is the only creation who has taken over attributes of Allah and, like Him, gathered opposites in himself. Hence he is designated as the most honorable in all creation.

Human being are equipped not only with positive inner potential to improve their moral standing, but also negative desires which may cause them to fall to the lowest depths of immorality. In this context, throughout their lives human beings witness a vehement conflict between these two poles. This micro-level conflict is actually a reflection of the micro-cosmos of the human being, and of the ongoing conflict in the universe. Real courage, which makes a person a decent human being, lies in the ability to obtain a positive result from inner conflict and preserve one's original, inborn morality.

Hence the name "perfect man" (*insān kāmil*) is commonly given to those who have achieved protection of the divine aspects in their nature. Such people are figures of extraordinary kindness and sincerity. They are the foreword and summary of the book of the universe, the stage upon which the essence of creation is shown.

Even the body of the perfect man reflects the purity of his heart due to his exceptional command over his organs. His heart has become the home of divine love and the magnificent palace

The Perfect Man

of knowledge of Allah (*ma'rifat Allāh*). Hence the heart of the perfect man, in a sense, becomes the proper home of Allah Almighty (*bayt Allāh*).

It is extremely difficult to fully analyse and explain the perfect man. Shaykh Sa'dī says, "The heart is the locus of Allah's revelation of Himself."

The words of the perfect man hide hidden spiritual meanings and his actions reflect perfection because he has benefited from the spiritual climate of the noble Prophet (upon him blessings and peace). His heart has become a locus of beauty, because reaching the Truth (*Haqq*) and becoming the vicegerent of Allah Almighty (*khalīfat Allāh*) is possible only through possessing a spiritually sound heart.

The perfect man embraces the true essence of the formula, "*Sharī'ah* (religious law) is my words, *tarīqah* (path) is my actions, and *haqīqah* (reality) is my states." One of the Prophets related that Allah said, *"Neither the heavens nor the earth can contain Me but the heart of My pious servant can contain Me."*[3]

The perfect man is the person who has lost his own will due to his love for Allah, like the moth which goes around the fire. Allah becomes his sight and hearing. Whatever was predestined for him becomes the most beautiful possibility for the perfect man. As he is looking at the divine view all the time, his love for this world is eliminated. All temporary gains have lost their significance.

---

3. Imam Ahmad narrates in *Kitab al-Zuhd* (Makkah al-Mukarramah ed. p. 81) from Wahb ibn Munabbih that Allah opened the heavens for Hizqil (Ezekiel) until he saw the Throne, whereupon Hizqil said, "How perfect You are! How Mighty You are, Lord!" Allah said, *"Truly, the heavens and the earth are too weak to contain Me, but the soft, humble heart of my believing servant can contain Me."*

The perfect man is in the state of watching and appreciating the divine beauty, the perfect order of the universe. The universe and the events that take place in it teach him countless lessons. He is in the state of the true consciousness of a humble believer who feels his insignificance and weakness in relation to the enduring divine revelation. This is why, most of the time, Allah Almighty accepts the prayers and requests of the perfect man, and does not reject them. His modesty and sincerity mean that he avoids desiring anything for his own personal benefit in his prayers; the seed of mercy molds his character and his heart cares for all creatures. He is completely aware of the fact that the universe is functioning in a perfect manner and surrounded by divine wisdom (*hikmah*). The divine rule in the universe is the best for us.

One day Sunbul Sinan Efendi asked his disciples, "If you were entitled to administrate the universe, what would you do?" On being asked such an unusual question his disciples were hesitant to answer. One said, "I would not leave a single unbeliever on earth!" Another said, "I would eliminate all evil from the earth." Some suggested punishing all drunken people. One of the disciples was waiting in silence, which attracted the attention of the shaikh. "O my son, what would you do?" he asked him.

He humbly replied, "O my Shaikh! This question implies that – may Allah forgive me – there is deficiency or imperfection in the administration of creation. How dare I, with my limited intellect, suggest any option other than the one already in place?"

Having heard this wise and perceptive answer, the Shaikh said, "The issue is now settled, we found the core of the issue."

The Perfect Man

After that event this disciple came to be known as Merkez Efendi. Eventually his real name, Musa Muslihiddin, was forgotten, and he is known today by the name *Merkez* ("Core").

Since the perfect man is completely aware of Allah's love, there is no chance for temptation to reside in his heart. Due to his being the center of spiritual attraction, people naturally find themselves in love and respect for him. This, however, does not make the perfect man arrogant or proud of himself.

He is constantly aware of Allah Almighty, even while he is among people, and obeys Allah's commands. He places great importance upon the commandments of Allah (*ta'zīm li-amr Allāh*)' and shows compassion and affection toward the creatures of Allah (*shafaqah li-khalq Allāh*)'. He loves all creatures but does not feel any sympathy towards wrongdoers and oppressors. However, out of his sense of mercy he also feels sorry for them. The only worldly possessions he requires are those needed to serve the needy and the poor.

The perfect man devotes himself to gaining knowledge of Allah and reaching Him, in accordance with the postulate "the human being is the secret of Me and I am the secret of the human being." The perfect man is now a servant who does not care about the grief and troubles of this world.

In a story it is said that Jesus (upon him blessings and peace) met a person whose body was covered in spots and he was perspiring constantly. Despite these troubles, the person would say:

"O my Lord! Infinite thanks and praise are due to You for Your saving me from the agonies You inflicted upon most of mankind."

In order to test his maturity and awareness, Jesus (upon him blessings and peace) asked him: "O man! What agony did Allah take away from you?"

The man replied: "O spirit of Allah! The most agonising illness and trouble is deprivation and ignorance of the Truth. All praise is due to Allah for protecting me from this. For I am in a state of joy and happiness due to the pardon He has bestowed upon me. No other worldly benefit is comparable to this."

The perfect man considers this world in light of the reality that everything will perish. He will be together with his Lord in the station of wonderment.

The sole aim and purpose of the perfect man is to achieve the satisfaction of Allah. On this path, sweet or bitter food are the same to him. Likewise, there is no difference in his view between much and little, warm and cold, or wealth and poverty; all are relative to him.

The perfect man appears to be a stranger to this world. In fact, the entire world means nothing to him but a game played in a sandbox. Hence, there is no demand that comes from fellow human beings or the world, to which his *nafs* will turn. He is modest in all of his affairs. He follows the best path in his worship.

A human being owes certain rights to his Lord, such as worship and thanksgiving. He owes his family and himself certain other rights. The perfect man maintains a balance between these obligations.

The perfect man is a gentle soul. He always keeps his promises and never breaks his word. He will not hurt another person in order to gain some personal interest. He is just in his conduct towards both his fellow human beings and Allah Almighty.

Even actions which are against his own interest will not distress him. If the offender is a person whom he used to help, the perfect man will continue acting benevolently to this person. Since a perfect man emulates the conduct of Allah and seeks only His satisfaction, his acts and behavior will naturally be compliant with the Qur'an and Sunnah. For Allah continues to sustain all creatures, even those ignorant ones who disobey Him.

The first of the Righteous Caliphs, Abū Bakr (may Allah be pleased with him), used to give charity to a certain man named Mistah bin Uthāthah, but he later found out that that man was involved in the case of slander (*ifk*) against his daughter 'Ā'isha, the wife of the Prophet (upon him blessings and peace). So Abū Bakr swore not to give Mistah anything anymore. Mistah's family became helpless and desperate. However, Allah Almighty, out of His benevolence even towards those who oppose Him, revealed the following verses:

وَلَا يَأْتَلِ أُولُوا الْفَضْلِ مِنكُمْ وَالسَّعَةِ أَن يُؤْتُوا أُولِي الْقُرْبَىٰ وَالْمَسَاكِينَ وَالْمُهَاجِرِينَ فِي سَبِيلِ اللَّهِ ۖ وَلْيَعْفُوا وَلْيَصْفَحُوا ۗ أَلَا تُحِبُّونَ أَن يَغْفِرَ اللَّهُ لَكُمْ ۗ وَاللَّهُ غَفُورٌ رَّحِيمٌ

Let not those among you who are endued with grace and amplitude of means resolve by oath against helping their kinsmen, those in want, and those who have left their homes in Allah's cause. Let them forgive and forbear. Do you not love that Allah should forgive you? For Allah is oft-forgiving, most merciful. (Nūr, 24:22)

وَلَا تَجْعَلُوا اللَّهَ عُرْضَةً لِّأَيْمَانِكُمْ أَن تَبَرُّوا وَتَتَّقُوا وَتُصْلِحُوا بَيْنَ النَّاسِ ۗ وَاللَّهُ سَمِيعٌ عَلِيمٌ

> *And make not Allah's (name) an excuse in your oaths against doing good, or acting rightly, or making peace between persons; for Allah is one who heareth and knoweth all things. (Baqara, 2:224)*

After the revelation of this verse, Abū Bakr (may Allah be pleased with him) said: "I of course love that Allah should forgive me." He then paid compensation for breaking oath, and resumed giving charity to the person who had falsely accused the wife of the Prophet and the mother of the believers, 'Ā'isha (may Allah be pleased with her). This, too, is the most outstanding example, and Abū Bakr's merit and perfection are rare indeed.

The perfect man spends so much for the sake of Allah in the right time and place that people may think him extravagant. If it is not the right time and right place, he gives so little that people may imagine that he is a stingy and mean person. However he lives solely for the sake of the truth. In the following verse of the Qur'an, Allah commands:

وَآتِ ذَا الْقُرْبَىٰ حَقَّهُ وَالْمِسْكِينَ وَابْنَ السَّبِيلِ وَلَا تُبَذِّرْ تَبْذِيرًا

إِنَّ الْمُبَذِّرِينَ كَانُوا إِخْوَانَ الشَّيَاطِينِ وَكَانَ الشَّيْطَانُ لِرَبِّهِ كَفُورًا

> *And give his due to the near of kin, as well as to the needy and the wayfarer, but do not squander [your substance] senselessly. Behold, the squanderers are, indeed, of the ilk of the satans - inasmuch as Satan has indeed proved most ungrateful to his Lord. (Isrā', 17:26-27).*

وَلَا تَجْعَلْ يَدَكَ مَغْلُولَةً إِلَىٰ عُنُقِكَ وَلَا تَبْسُطْهَا كُلَّ الْبَسْطِ فَتَقْعُدَ مَلُومًا مَّحْسُورًا

The Perfect Man

Make not your hand tied (like a niggard's) to your neck, nor stretch it forth to its utmost reach, so that you become blameworthy and destitute. (Isrā', 17:29)

'Umar b. 'Abd al-'Azīz, who understood the verse very well, distributed to the needy and the orphans from his own possessions and the wealth of his family with their consent. He became a role model for his subjects. Since the rich people in his reign followed him by example, there remained no poor in his time that would qualify for *zakâh*. He also set a shining precedent against extravagance by living in a tent instead of a palace.

The perfect man always controls his *nafs*. He has no interest in the shortcomings and deficiencies of other people. He does not pay attention to the secrets of others and does not disclose them. The perfect man emulates Allah's attribute *sattār al-'uyūb* (the One who covers mistakes).

Living a content life without any hankering after the temporary pleasures of this world, the perfect man holds a lofty status which everybody envies. Even the world was ordered to obey him. A hadīth states:

Whoever cares mostly about the hereafter, Allah will make him wealthy of heart, give his actions order and strength and the world will come to him in surrender. But whoever cares mostly about this world, Allah will put his poverty in front of his eyes and make him a vagrant. He will only receive what is preordained for him in this world. (Tirmidhi)

The perfect man has obtained such a high rank of character and nature that he does not get angry or upset by anyone except for the sake of Allah. He puts into practice the meaning of the divine expression:

الَّذِينَ يُنفِقُونَ فِي السَّرَّاءِ وَالضَّرَّاءِ وَالْكَاظِمِينَ الْغَيْظَ وَالْعَافِينَ عَنِ النَّاسِ وَاللَّهُ يُحِبُّ الْمُحْسِنِينَ

Those who spend (freely), whether in prosperity or in adversity, who restrain anger, and pardon (all) men; for Allah loves those who do good. (Āl 'Imrān, 3:134)

Ja'far al-Sādiq, practising the essence of this verse, forgave his servant who had spilled food on his clothes, and treated him well. Al-Hasan al-Basrī used to forgive those who would backbite him, and he would educate them by sending them gifts.

The perfect man is always in the state of kindness and worship. His breaths are in glorification of Allah (*tasbīh*). His words spread pearls of wisdom. His eyes are a fountain of enlightenment (*fayd*) and love (*mahabba*). He makes people remember Allah through his presence. Those who attend his friendly circles live in ecstasy with the enjoyment and delight they have experienced because his conversation is full of joy. He conveys many spiritual bestowals according to the ability of his audience. He is the interpreter of the truth for those who are anxious to receive divine mysteries.

Allah Almighty loves the man who has attained this conduct and brings other people to love him too. In turn, this person will guide the seekers of the path of Allah with grace and sincerity. He will sacrifice himself in order to rescue the people around him from the horrible darkness of ego (*nafs*) to the light of the Heavens. The Prophet (upon him blessings and peace), who suffered the most severe hardship in this attempt, thus said: "Those who endure the severest trials are the Prophets, then those who resemble them most" (Tirmidhī).

The Perfect Man

The perfect man is a treasury of divine secrets. Only those who are familiar with the divine secrets will be able to appreciate his perfection, since a perfect man is not outwardly different from other people. However, he is a person whose soul has been perfected by Allah. He represents the secret of *ahsani taqwīm* (the most excellent pattern). He is a mine of light, a diamond attached to the chains of good people from the Prophet's time to the present day. The inheritance of Khidr who had access to the divine (*ladunnī*) knowledge is bestowed upon him.

The soul of the perfect man will not perish when he is buried under the soil; the product of his soul will survive forever. Such nobles as Shāh-i Naqshband, al-Ghazālī, Mawlānā Rūmī and Adabali continue to this day the services they began in this world. They still live among us and will continue to live after we die.

To attain the meeting with Allah hardly occurs with the help of power or the capital of reputation; rather, it is the result of a spiritual life. That is why Allah Almighty provided the perfect man with the happiness of two worlds by protecting him from fear and sadness here and hereafter. He says:

أَلَا إِنَّ أَوْلِيَاءَ اللَّهِ لَا خَوْفٌ عَلَيْهِمْ وَلَا هُمْ يَحْزَنُونَ

Behold! Verily on the friends of Allah there is no fear, nor shall they grieve." (*Yūnus*, 10:62)

In the history of the dignity of mankind there always stand perfect people. It was their guidance that led those who would eventually be the world conquerors to hold the power. In this respect, the first three centuries of the Ottoman State is full of perfect men like Shaykh Adabali and others that come from this blessed chain. They filled their environment with guidance and abundant blessings. They directed their community from a spiritual world. One of the best examples of Ottoman Sultans is Sultan Yavuz Selim. Despite being a mighty ruler, he preferred to serve Islam and the friends of Allah to being a king. He mentioned this in a poem:

To be a world conqueror is a meaningless fight,
To be a servant to a walī (a friend of Allah) is above all.

We pray to Allah to give us poor and weak the same zeal of love that He bestowed on Sultan Yavuz. We remember with prayer and ask the mercy of Allah for the perfect man and great *walī*, Sultān al-'Ārifīn, Mahmud Sami Ramazanoğlu (may his soul be sanctified), who gave us great benefit through his spiritual benevolence. We also ask for Allah to give healing and many years of guidance for the successor of this great *walī*, Musa Topbaş Efendi.[4]

---

4. Ustādh Musa Topbaş Efendi was ill when these pages were written and he passed away in 1999.

3.

Standing firm on the path of Allah

Istiqāmah (standing firm) literally means "continuous, fearless and unwavering progression towards a target." In Sufi terminology it corresponds to "the ability of preserving the innocence and purity of our nature (the state in which we are created) without damage and destruction."

As a result of the protection of the spiritual life of the heart, the *nafs* (lower self) attains *adab* (good character) as the heart draws nearer to spirituality so as to achieve *akhlāq Muhammadiyyah* (the character of Muhammad, upon him blessings and peace). Secrets begin to become evident; Allah the Almighty becomes the very goal of goals; *mā siwā* or anything else besides Allah loses its significance, and the believer enters a state where he or she can reach the divine presence.

In order to emphasize how difficult it is to achieve this state, the Prophet (upon him blessings and peace) – even though he is the *sine qua non* of creation, a mercy to all being, as well as the best example of perfection in morality – was addressed in a divine warning to "Therefore stand firm (in the straight path) as you are commanded." (*Hūd*, 11:112)

Indeed the Prophet (upon him blessings and peace) feeling the enormous burden in responsibility of his divine mission, said: "The chapter of *Hūd* made me older." The Companions asked him: "O Messenger of Allah! Is it the stories of the prophets that made you old?" The Prophet (upon him blessings and peace) replied: "It was the verse which states, "Therefore stand firm (in the straight path) as you are commanded" (*Hūd*, 11:112). After the revelation of this verse, there appeared some whiteness in the hair of Allah's Messenger (upon him blessings and peace) which had previously been a pure jet black without any white at all. Commentators explain this verse in the following way:

> *O Prophet! You must be a model of uprightness by behaving in accordance with Qur'anic morals and principles so that there will not be any doubt about you! Do not mind the words of hypocrites and pagans, leave them to Allah! Be upright in your private and public duties as you have been commanded, and do not stray from the right path! However difficult it is to remain on the right path, do not be daunted by any hindrance in the way of carrying out and applying this command! Your Lord is your helper.*

In this connection Abd Allāh b. 'Abbās said, "No other commandment weighed more heavily upon the Prophet's (upon him blessings and peace) shoulders than this verse in the Qur'an."

On the other hand, this verse addresses all Muslims in the person of the Prophet (upon him blessings and peace). So then, what made the Prophet (upon him blessings and peace) older was his concern about his community (*ummah*) since this command addresses them all. For his own righteousness is confirmed by the following verse:

عَلَىٰ صِرَاطٍ مُّسْتَقِيمٍ إِنَّكَ لَمِنَ الْمُرْسَلِينَ

"*You are indeed one of the messengers, on a straight way.*" (*Yāsīn*, 36:3-4)

Therefore there is not any other way to reach Allah except to be on the straight path, and there is not any other command more difficult than to stay on the straight path. The highest station on the Sufi path is to ensure that one follows the straight path in every matter. It is because of this difficulty that this command has been presented in the oft-repeated Surah *Fātihah* in the form of a prayer. The repetition of the prayer "Show us the straight way" (Fātihah, 1:6) by Muslims dozens of times every day illustrates how difficult it is to stay on the straight path.

The straight path is referred to in the Qur'an as the path of Allah, the proper way, the book of Allah, faith and issues related to faith, Islam and *Sharīʿah*, the path of the Prophet Muhammad (upon him blessings and peace) and his Companions, the path of the righteous and the martyrs, the road of happiness in this world and the hereafter, the path of Paradise, etc.

So the straight path is the path of the chosen people who have been blessed by Allah. These are first the prophets, then the most-truthful, the martyrs, and the righteous people. All that follow are also people of the straight path. The straight path is the way that takes the believer to Allah. Allah the Almighty says: "The path of Allah, to Whom belongs whatever is in the heavens and whatever is on earth. Behold (how) all affairs tend towards Allah!" (*Shūrā*, 42: 53)

To be on the straight path is only possible through worshipping and serving Allah: "It is Allah Who is my Lord and your Lord; then worship Him. This is a way that is straight." (*Āl ʿImrān*, 3:51) "Whoever holds firmly to Allah will be shown a way that is straight." (*Āl ʿImrān*, 3:101).

The straight path is defined in Sūrah *Anʿām* in the following way:

Say: "Come, I will rehearse what Allah has (really) prohibited you from": join not anything with Him: Be good to your parents; kill not your children on the pretext of poverty. We provide sustenance for you and for them. Come not near indecent deeds, whether open or secret; take not life, which Allah has made sacred, except by way of justice and law: Thus He commands you, that you may learn wisdom. And come not near to the orphan's property, except to improve it, until he attain the age of full strength; give measure and weight with (full) justice; no burden do We place on any soul, but that which it can bear. Whenever you speak, speak justly, even if a near relative is concerned; and fulfil the covenant of Allah. Thus He commands you, that you may remember. Verily, this is My way leading straight. Follow it. Follow not (other) paths. They will scatter you about from His path. Thus He commands you, that you may be righteous. (An'ām, 6:151-153)

Man cannot achieve the straight path properly unless he or she prefers the love of Allah (*mahabbat Allāh*) over the love of other beings. To reach this station, man needs to know Allah as He deserves to be known. Hence it can be said that the straight path is *ma'rifat Allāh* (knowledge of Allah). Because whoever attains this knowledge and arranges his or her life in accordance with it, escapes from the evils of his or her nature and from the wiles of Satan. A person's heart at this stage is rewarded with spiritual blessings. He or she opens a window to spiritual worlds; and the universe turns into a great book filled with wisdom.

Abū Sa'īd al-Kharrāz, one of the people of *ma'rifah*, saw Satan in his dream and tried to hit him with his stick. Iblīs said, "O Abū Sa'īd! I do not fear your stick; for this stick is visible. What I fear is the luminous lights of the sun of spiritual knowledge that rises from the skies of the *ārif*'s (knower's) heart and burns and destroys all of the *mā siwā*."

On the Sufi path, the endeavors of a *murīd* (disciple) without uprightness (i.e. following the straight path) are in vain. His efforts give him no benefit at all. That is why standing firm in the path of Allah is accepted as the greatest miracle. According to another definition, the "straight path" means maintaining moderation in all actions without going to extremes (like spending too much or too little), and persevering on the right path, obeying the divine commands as they have been given.

The Messenger of Allah (upon him blessings and peace) commands the believers to act in moderation. It should be known that the Prophet (upon him blessings and peace) lived all of his life in accordance with this rule, and within the limits of a human being in order to become an example for the others. His life is the best example of worshipping Allah, respecting the rights of the family members and all other social interactions. The messenger of Allah (upon him blessings and peace) has given all these acts their rightful place and presented their arrangements to his *ummah*. To depart from the teachings of the Prophet (upon him blessings and peace) and neglect some duties while following others in an extreme way is therefore not an acceptable manner. We must arrange our lives in accordance with the norms offered by the Prophet (upon him blessings and peace) not in accordance with our subjective desires.

The great Sufi master 'Abd al-Khāliq Ghujduwānī explained this point clearly. He was once asked, "Shall we do what our ego-*nafs* desires or shall we do what it does not like?" The Sheikh replied, "It is very difficult to distinguish between the two. *Nafs* usually deceives people whether the desires are divine or satanic. Because of this, it is enough to follow the commandments of Allah and refrain from His prohibitions. This is true servitude."

Allah states: "Say: 'This is my way; I do invite unto Allah, with a certain knowledge I and whoever follows me. Glory to Allah! and never will I join gods with Allah!'" (*Yūsuf*, 12:108).

In the various ages of ignorance humankind went through, when people were slaves to material power and the desires of the *nafs*, some exceptionally pious men were charged with the duty of prophecy. These distinguished people who were the model for their communities were charged with three duties: 1) To recite the verses of Allah and announce them, 2) To teach the book and wisdom, 3) To purify their nature i.e. to give people proper guidance (*istiqāmah*).

Starting from Adam (upon him blessings and peace) this holy chain of prophethood came to full maturity with Prophet Muhammad (upon him blessings and peace). The straight path or *istiqāmah* is a collection of *'amal sālih* or good deeds.

In order to consider an action *'amal sālih*, there are two conditions:

1. *Ta'zīm li-amr Allāh* or to follow Allah's commands properly and in humility

2. *Shafaqat li-khalq Allāh* or to love, show affection and be generous to creatures for the sake of their Creator.

In other words, uprightness is to love the Messenger of Allah and to receive a share of his model personality and exemplary morality, to live in accordance with the spiritual guidance of the Qur'an and Sunnah, to stay away from worldy pleasures, and to reach the secrets of worship, servitude and knowledge. It is necessary for a person to keep his or her internal world under control in order to recognize truth and uprightness. Deviation from performing actions for the sake of Allah means insincerity, which completely devalues those actions in the presence of Allah. That is why actions have to be performed just for the sake of Allah.

Even 'Umar b. al-Khattāb (may Allah be pleased with him) worried about the preservation of sincerity and uprightness in his life. When he came to power he said:

"O People! If I deviated from the path of Allah or incline to wrongdoing what would you do?"

A Bedouin stood up and said:

"O Caliph! Do not worry, if you incline to wrongdoing we will straighten you with our swords!" The Caliph 'Umar, pleased with this response, thanked Allah:

"All praises are to You my Lord! You have blessed me with a community who would bring me back to the straight path if I deviated!"

The Prophet (upon him blessings and peace) informed only Hudhayfa of those who had the sign of hypocrisy in their hearts for the safety of the Muslim *ummah*. 'Umar heard this, and one day asked Hudhayfa:

"O Hudhayfa! For the sake of Allah, tell me, is there any sign of hypocrisy in me?"

Hudhayfa replied saying:

"O Caliph! I can guarantee only to you that you do not have any signs of hypocrisy!"

Al-Hasan al-Basrī said to his disciple Tāwūs, who was a hadith teacher:

"O Tāwūs! If you take pride in teaching hadith, give up teaching this discipline!"

Al-Ghazālī, when teaching three hundred students, was worried about himself:

"Do I seek Allah's favor when teaching these students, or am I in danger of being corrupted by love of fame?"

After that al-Ghazālī distributed his wealth, gave up teaching, and lived in seclusion. Consequently, the Prophet's spirituality manifested itself to him and he attained ease of heart. Finally, he transformed into a completely different Ghazālī. Only then did he resume teaching.

Sultan Yavuz Selim on his way back from his campaign in Egypt learned that people in Istanbul were waiting for him with great excitement. Because of this, although he came very close to the city, he camped his army at the foot of Camlica hill and did not enter Istanbul. He was concerned that he would be defeated by his *nafs*, and said to his manservant Hasan Can:

"Let's wait until getting dark when everybody goes home; then we will enter Istanbul. Do not let the compliments and applause of people, and the pride of victory knock us down!"

Finally he entered the city secretly, avoiding the applause and praise of the people. All of these examples teach us that we should stand firm on the straight path under all circumstances, and that we should cleanse our hearts from all kinds of impurities.

The heart is the locus in which the divine is manifested. The value of worship depends on the clarity of heart. The Qur'an says: "The day whereon neither wealth nor sons will avail, but only he (will prosper) that brings to Allah a sound heart" (*Shu'arā'*, 26:88-89). Likewise the Prophet (upon him blessings and peace) says, "Truly Allah does not look at your appearance and your possessions; but He looks at your hearts and your deeds" (*Sahih Muslim*).

I pray to Allah that He gives us the power and will to stand firm on the straight path.

Amin!

4.

Being with the righteous and the truthful

Once there was a heedless man who hated the friends of Allah. One day he passed by a dervish sheikh's convent and wondered what was inside. He sneaked in and saw the dervishes gathered, listening to a *suhbah* or talk. The heedless man belittled their state and went on his way.

That night he saw a terrifying nightmare. It was the Day of the Last Judgement and demons were taking him to Hell. At that moment the Sheikh from the convent appeared and told the demons:

"Leave him alone, yesterday he showed up in our gathering."

The demons replied:

"But he is a heedles man and deserves Hell!"

Just then, the man woke up. The first thing he did in the morning was to go to the convent and join the fellowship of the wise.

According to a hadith reported by Anas b. Mālik (may Allah be pleased with him), there are groups of angels that roam the earth looking for *dhikr* gatherings. When they find one, they circle around it and say:

"O Lord! Those servants of Yours are reading Your book, saying praises upon Your Prophet and asking from You their needs both in this world and in the hereafter.

Allah Almighty says:

Being with the righteous and the truthful

"Be witnesses I forgive them all."

The angels say:

"O Lord! So-and-so was in this gathering by mistake."

Allah Almighty replies:

"They (righteous and truthful servants) are such a group that people who are with them will not be considered disobedient."

The good tidings in the above mentioned reports encourage Muslims to be with the righteous and the truthful. On the Sufi path, it is necessary to be with the righteous and the truthful in order to benefit from their spirituality and protect the heart from *mā siwā*. Unlike other organs of the body, the heart operates involuntarily and it easily tends to assimilate its surroundings.

The heart easily takes on the color and characteristics of its surroundings. The influence of the environment can be either positive or negative. If the heart does not get the proper education and obtain a certain level of control, it faces serious dangers. Controlling love and hatred have determining effects on spiritual ascension or descent.

It is very important on the way of spiritual perfection to love what deserves to be loved and hate what deserves to be hated.

The importance of being with the righteous and truthful servants of Allah and living in their circle of influence is considerable for spiritual progress. However, the level of benefit depends upon the level of love for the beloved. Otherwise, just being together produces little outcome despite some benefits.

It is noteworthy that the words *sahābī* (Companion of the Prophet Muhammad, upon him blessings and peace) and *suhbah* (gathering) come from the same Arabic root. Indeed, the Companions exemplify the ones who benefited most from the *suhbah* of the Prophet through their abundant love and respect for him. In order to understand how they climbed so high in the spiritual realm we must see how they respected the Prophet (upon him blessings and peace). A *sahābī* states: "We listened to the Prophet's (upon him blessings and peace) talk with such care that as if there were birds on our heads we feared lest they would fly away if we moved."

The Prophet (upon him blessings and peace) watered the Companions' parched hearts with the rains of wisdom and mercy. Thanks to being with the Prophet, seeds of wisdom and knowledge leafed out from the soil of their hearts. The reflection of love and spirituality of the Prophet in their hearts produced their exemplary new personalities. The old personality of the *Jāhiliyyah* (the age of ignorance before Islam), who buried daughters alive and committed all other sorts of merciless acts, disappeared. In the very same bodies, crying, gentle, selfless and sensitive characters were formed.

They carried the paradigmatic life of the Prophet (upon him blessings and peace) everywhere they went. Narrations from their virtuous lives will show humanity the straight path forever. Allah Almighty praises the Companions with the following words:

وَالسَّابِقُونَ الْأَوَّلُونَ مِنَ الْمُهَاجِرِينَ وَالْأَنْصَارِ وَالَّذِينَ اتَّبَعُوهُم بِإِحْسَانٍ رَّضِيَ اللَّهُ عَنْهُمْ وَرَضُواْ عَنْهُ وَأَعَدَّ لَهُمْ جَنَّاتٍ تَجْرِي تَحْتَهَا الْأَنْهَارُ خَالِدِينَ فِيهَا أَبَدًا ذَٰلِكَ الْفَوْزُ الْعَظِيمُ

The vanguard (of Islam)—the first of those who forsook (their homes) and those who gave them aid, and (also) those who follow them in (all) good deeds, well-pleased is Allah with them, as are they with Him. For them has He prepared gardens under which rivers flow, to dwell therein for ever. That is the supreme triumph. (Tawba, 9:100)

Being with the righteous and the truthful

The sermons and *suhbah*s (conversations and gatherings) of the believers borrow their beauty from the beauty of the Prophet's (upon him blessings and peace) *suhbah*s. It is the Prophet's (upon him blessings and peace) light that is reflected in the words of the scholars and friends of Allah. Muslims should be aware of the significance of those gatherings, because they are like the gardens of Paradise in which there are eyes and hearts crying for the love of Allah. We must attend such circles and try to be with the pious (*sālih*) and the truthful (*sādiq*) believers. This is the only way we can develop our spiritual well-being and adorn our hearts with the best qualities.

If a believer wants to protect his or her spiritual development from negative influences then he/she should avoid being with the sinners and the heedless. The wind blowing over a carrion or dumping ground spreads its repulsive smell everywhere it blows. Concerning this, Sheikh 'Ubayd Allāh Ahrār warns his followers, "Companionship with sinners brings tension, desolation and lack of concentration to the heart."

One day Abū Yazīd al-Bistāmī felt wretchedness in his heart. He could not concentrate his mind and asked the friends in his circle: "Is there anyone in our company who is a stranger (a sinner)?" His friends looked around but could not find anyone they did not know.

Abū Yazīd insisted: "Look carefully! Check the area where the walking sticks are kept. There is the trace of a sinner in this meeting. Otherwise, I would not feel so uneasy and cheerless."

They searched around once more and found the stick of a sinner. They threw it outside. Abū Yazīd found his peace of mind and his spiritual rapture came back.

On another occasion, 'Ubayd Allāh Ahrār said to one of his close companions: "I feel something wrong with you. I think you are wearing the garment of a stranger." His companion said with astonishment: "Indeed I am," then he changed his garment and came back.

A different example of this can be found in the story of the Prophet Joseph and his father Jacob (upon them blessings and peace). The latter loved his son more than his other children, because he saw his own characteristics in Joseph. His love for him was so intense that when Joseph's shirt was sent to him nobody else but he could sense his smell.

If the spiritual states of the friends of Allah penetrate even the nature of material things, how much more significant is it to scrupulously take care of the heart, which is undoubtedly more sensitive than material things? The leading figures of the Sufi path say:

> *Even unliving beings are affected by the actions and morals of people. Praying in a place where all sorts of sins were committed is very different from praying in a place where good deeds were performed. For this reason, the reward of a prayer performed in the Ka'ba is greater than the prayer performed anywhere else.*

We can gather another example from the life of the Prophet (upon him blessings and peace). One day when he (upon him blessings and peace) was passing through the valley of Muhassir, which is a place between Arafat and Muzdalifah, he started to speed up his walk. The Companions wondered, "Messenger of Allah, why did you start rushing all of a sudden?" He answered:

Being with the righteous and the truthful

"Allah Almighty destroyed the tyrant Abrahah and his army at this place."

On another occasion, the Prophet (upon him blessings and peace) was returning from the campaign of Tabūk. The Companions were very tired, so they wanted to have a rest. They stopped at the place the nation of Thamūd had once inhabited. The Prophet (upon him blessings and peace) said, "Allah Almighty destroyed the nation of Thamūd here. Do not take any water from this place so that their grief will not affect you." They said: "Messenger of Allah! We have already kneaded the dough with its water, and also filled our bags with its water." Upon that, the Prophet ordered them to feed the camels with the dough and pour out the water." (Bukhārī, Anbiyā', 17)

These and similar *aḥādīth* show that even inanimate objects are influenced by the good or bad incidents that took place around them.

Likewise, the friends of Allah spread their spiritual blessings, their love and ecstasy to the people in their gatherings. The light in their hearts is reflected in the others. We should not forget that as material things influence each other, similarly spiritual circumstances and objects affect others. To the extent of its reflection and transformation, the heart gets filled with wisdom and truth, just like the morning breeze carries the sweet smell of roses, musk and other fragrances wherever it blows. Hence we must do our best to benefit from the spiritual perfection and the good states of the righteous and the truthful. Concerning this Allah the Exalted states in the Qur'an:

يَا أَيُّهَا الَّذِينَ آمَنُوا اتَّقُوا اللَّهَ وَكُونُوا مَعَ الصَّادِقِينَ

"O you who believe! Fear Allah and be with those who are truthful." (Tawba, 9:119)

In order to perfect one's faith, one needs to befriend those who are honest in their words and deeds and truthful to Allah in their loyalty and love. If we love such friends of Allah we can more easily attain the spiritual stations they have reached. One day a man asked Abū Yazīd, "Advise me of a good deed which would bring me closer to Allah." Abū Yazīd answered, "Love the friends of Allah and they will love you too. Try to find a place in their hearts. For Allah looks into the hearts of His friends three-hundred and sixty times a day. If he finds your name in one of their hearts, He will forgive you."

For that reason, in Sufi training, *rābitah* (connection) establishes a spiritual link between disciple and master of the path. When the disciple establishes this link with the friend of Allah (whom he has accepted as his model), his love and obedience to his advice are always kept in mind. Through *rābitah* the disciple attains perfect affinity with his master, and he or she may gain all sorts of spiritual blessings.

Rābitah, with the intensity of love, creates high spiritual sensitivity in the heart. Through this sensitivity the disciple starts to advance in the path of "sameness" (*'ayniyyah*) with the master.

Through love and spiritual attachment, the lover loses himself in his beloved. Jalāl al-Dīn Rūmī explains this state in the following way:

When the river meets the sea it becomes the sea. It is no longer a river. The bread we eat is dissolved in our stomach, and becomes part of our body. Similarly, the lover is annihilated in his beloved to the extent of his love for the beloved.

Rūmī explains this state of annihilation saying:

Love filled my veins and skin like blood. It took me from myself, and filled my existence with affection. My friend covered all of the parts of my body. The only thing left from me is my name the rest is He...

This is known in *tasawwuf* as *fanā' fī Allāh* and *baqā' bi-Allāh*, annihilation in Allah and eternal union with Him, respectively. However, it is not an easy task to be able to possess love for Allah directly, without undertaking the necessary spiritual practices. The heart needs to be ready to bear such a heavy state.

Abū Bakr (may Allah be pleased with him) loved the Prophet (upon him blessings and peace) very much. Even in his presence his love and longing for him were increasing instead of decreasing. When he gave away all his possessions and his wealth, the Prophet praised him. Abū Bakr said, "O Prophet of Allah, may my life, my wealth, my everything be ransomed for you!" Rūmī, reflecting on this very idea, says, "What is gold, what is life, what are pearls and jewels if they are not spent in the way of the beloved?"

It is narrated that Abū Bakr said on the pulpit that even in the places of washing and cleaning he felt shy before Allah. It is in return for this excessive love that the Prophet (upon him blessings and peace) said on his deathbed, "Let all the doors be closed except the door of Abū Bakr."[5]

---

5. Some people at that time had private doors opening to the masjid and the Prophet wanted them to be closed, only excepting Abū Bakr's door so as to honor him.

Sheikh Sa'dī Shirāzī explains the mutual influence of the states as follows:

The dog of the companions of the cave was honored by being with them. It is even mentioned in the Qur'an and became part of history. However, Lot's (upon him blessings and peace) wife chose to be with sinners and infidels.

Sheikh Sa'dī metaphorically explains the achievement of "sameness and oneness" as a result of being with the righteous and the truthful in the following story:

"A man goes to bathhouse. One of his friends gives him scented clay to get cleaned. The nice smell of the clay spread to every part of the bathhouse. The man asked the clay:

- I love your smell; tell me, what are you, musk or amber?

The clay replied:

- I am neither musk nor amber, just ordinary soil. However, I was under a rose tree and got washed with its water. My scent comes from those roses."

As these examples clearly show, we must sincerely submit ourselves to the friends of Allah. In this way, we can reflect the divine lights which dwell in their hearts, just as the moon reflects the light of the sun.

O Lord! Resurrect us together with those who are truthful to You in their devotion and belief. Bestow upon us goodness linked to the gatherings of the Prophet and the Companions.

Amin!

5.

Sincerity towards Allah

Sincerity (*ikhlās*) is to protect one's heart from the thought of worldly interests when one performs a duty towards Allah the Almighty. The fruit of sincerity is *ihsān* – to worship Allah as if one can see Him, and to live with the awareness that Allah is watching one's actions at all times. Imam Qushayrī narrated the following account:

'Amr b. Layth was a commander of an army in Khurasān. After he passed away, a pious man saw him in his dream. He asked the army commander:

"How has Allah treated you?"

"Allah has forgiven all my sins."

"Why has Allah forgiven all your sins?"

'Amr replied:

"One day I climbed to the top of a tall hill and I looked down upon my army. Their strength and great number gave me great satisfaction, and I said to myself: 'I wish I could have joined the battles of the Prophet (upon him blessings and peace) with this well-trained army, and helped the Prophet (upon him blessings and peace) during his times of difficulty. I would have given my life to carry out this honor.' Because of these sincere feelings I had, Allah the Almighty forgave me and rewarded me with great things."

This incident is a good example of how sincere feelings and actions are rewarded. Even though the believer did not actualize his intention he was rewarded for his sincerity.

Concerning this, the Prophet (upon him blessings and peace) says that the intention of a believer is more valuable than his action. The value of the action comes from the good intention behind it. If there is no good intention behind a good act, it cannot be accepted as good. The Prophet (upon him blessings and peace) says, actions will be judged according to the intentions behind them:

> *The [reward of] deeds depends solely upon the intention and every person will get their reward according to what he or she has intended. So, whoever emigrated for Allah and His Apostle, then his emigration was for Allah and His Apostle. And whoever emigrated for worldly benefits or for a woman he meant to marry, his emigration was for what he emigrated for.*

Therefore we must always control our intentions when we perform an action. We must always aim to please Allah through our deeds. This quality is known as *ikhlās* (sincerity) in Islamic terminology. Actions are like the body and the intentions are like the soul. If the soul is ill, then so too is the body. Prayers and other religious activities which are not accompanied with sincere good intentions do not give any benefit to the person who performed them. They will only produce exhaustion. On the other hand, if a person aims to please Allah, even the most ordinary and trivial actions are rewarded by Allah the Almighty.

Mankind shares the characteristics of other living creatures in many respects. However, Man is different from them by the fact that he acts in such a way that he can save himself from the selfishness of his *nafs* and the cravings of his animal instincts. He can achieve domination over his base desires. In this way he can manifest the superiority over nature given to him by Allah. Once mankind achieves this state, all worldly actions such as sleeping, eating and drinking, getting married and having children, and all other acts, are in complete submission to the will of Allah. They are considered the deeds of mankind which are worthy of reward in the divine court.

Hence, a believer should cleanse his or her heart of all selfish intentions, leaving in his or her heart only the intention of attaining Allah's satisfaction. Through sincerity, a man or woman can come nearer to Allah.

The fruit of sincerity towards Allah is the station of *ihsān*. *Ihsān* means to worship Allah as if one sees Him, and to act accordingly, feeling His presence at all times. Behind all actions Allah asks sincerity towards Him: "Verily it is We Who have revealed the book to you in truth; so serve Allah, offering Him sincere devotion. Is it not to Allah that sincere devotion is due?" (*Zumar*, 39:2-3); "Say: Verily, I am commanded to worship Allah with sincere devotion." (*Zumar*, 39:11).

When Iblīs (Satan) was cast away from the divine presence he said: "O my Lord! Because You have put me in the wrong, I will make wrong fair-seeming to them on the earth, and I will put them all in the wrong, except Your chosen servants among them" (*Hijr*, 15:39-40). As the verse makes clear, Satan cannot influence the believers who are sincere to Allah in their devotion. Apart from them, all other believers are in danger. This fact is stated in the following verses: "This is for me a straight path. No authority shall you have over My servants, except such as put themselves in the wrong and follow you" (*Hijr*, 15:41-42).

In the chapter of *al-Isrā'*, this fact is again repeated: "As for my servants, no authority shall you have, except such as put themselves in the wrong and follow you." (*Isrā'*, 17:65)

In a hadith qudsī, Allah the Almighty says: "Sincerity is one of my divine secrets and I bestow it upon the servants whom I love. Neither an angel can discover it to record it, nor can a devil discover it in order to spoil it." (*Tāj*, I, 43)

This hadith indicates that a believer is endowed with sincerity if he has love in his heart for Allah. The phrase in the above hadith "the servants whom I love" shows that love is the preconditon of sincerity. The believers should place love for God in the highest place in their hearts. Consequently love should also be sincere. If love has no sincerity it will bring destruction to the lover as in the story narrated by Nakhshabī:

"One day a young man knocked at the door of the king's daughter and told her that he loved her. She told him to take a thousand *dirham*s (pounds) from her and go away and to disturb her anymore.

The young man did not give up and continued to come to her door.

She offered two thousand *dirham*s. In the end the young man accepted ten thousand *dirham*s in order to give up his love.

However, the real intention of the king's daughter was to test his sincerity in love. She asked him, 'What kind of love is yours that you prefer money over my love? Do you know the punishment for preferring something over me?' Then she commanded her soldiers to kill this young man who was not sincere in his love."

One of Nakhshabī's disciples was a deeply spiritual person, and when he heard this story he fell down. When he came back to his senses, he told his friends: "O my friends! Look at the punishment for false love in this world. Then consider the punishment of those who claim to love Allah and prefer trivial things over Him in the hereafter."

In that way, he gave us a good lesson on the significance of sincerity. Rūmī summarized the story saying: "A man's value is judged according to what he is looking for in life."

Sincerity is the most necessary condition of all the forms of worship. The Holy Qur'an states that only those who are sincere will be saved from their fate: "Most surely you will taste the painful punishment. But the chosen servants of Allah, for them is a sustenance determined, fruits; and they (shall enjoy) honor and dignity" (*Sâffât*, 37: 38-42).

"O you who believe! Guard your own souls: Follow right guidance. No hurt can come to you from those who stray. The return of you all is to Allah: it is He that will inform you of all that you do." (*Mā'idah*, 5:105)

Mawlānā Rūmī addresses those who pray without sincerity:

Would that, in your bowing low in prayer, you would turn your face (to attentive consideration) and apprehend the meaning of "Glory be unto my Lord! Who is the Most Exalted." Bow down with your heart, not only with your head. (Mathnawī, II, 1801)

As Rūmī emphasises, the important thing is that we prostrate ourselves in front of Allah with our hearts full of sincerity. Prayer has no value if it is contaminated by spiritual diseases such as hypocrisy. Allah the Almighty condemns such kinds of worship: "So woe to the worshippers who are neglectful of their prayers." (*Māʿūn*, 107:4-5)

Sincerity is to protect ourselves from making partners with Allah when we perform an action – to be sincere in our worship and not carry other any worldly intention when we do something for Allah. Hence we can describe righteous deeds as the sincere deeds. Sincere deeds are the ones which are cleansed of bad intentions. It is the pure milk which comes out of blood and feces.

And verily in cattle (too) will you find an instructive sign. From what is within their bodies, between excretions and blood, We produce, for your drink, milk, pure and agreeable to those who drink it."(Nahl, 16:66)

In contemplating the above verse the commentators of the holy Quran say that sincerity means purification of intentions from worldy concerns other than Allah, just as milk is pure and free from blood and excretions.

Junayd Baghdādī describes sincerity as the purification of deeds from any admixture of ostentation. However, claiming sincerity is not considered to be good behavior in Sufi circles. A friend of Allah once said: "To claim to be sincere is to be insincere."

Prophet Moses was commanded by Allah to choose seventy pious believers from his tribe. When he asked his people, three men came forward supposing themselves to be pious and sincere people. Upon this the following revelation came from Allah: O

Sincerity towards Allah

Moses! Those three men are the farthest from Me among My creation since they claimed to be pious and sincere.

The Prophet Jesus (upon him blessings and peace) was once asked about the definition of sincere deeds, and he answered, "To do deeds for the sake of Allah and not to expect any worldly rewards."

What is the biggest enemy of sincerity? It is hypocrisy, ostentation and showing off – to act in order to obtain worldly gain rather than for the pleasure of Allah. If deeds are done for other than Allah, then it is a hidden association of partners with Allah. The following hadith is very important in explaining the negative consequences of hypocrisy and showing off.

On the authority of Sulaymān b. Yasār it has been narrated: "People surrounded Abū Hurayra. Nātil, a Syrian, said to him, 'O Sheikh, relate (to us) a hadith you heard from the Messenger of Allah.' He replied, 'Yes. I heard the Messenger of Allah (upon him blessings and peace) say: 'The first of those men (whose case) will be decided on the Day of Judgement will be the man who died as a martyr. He shall be brought before the Judgement Seat and Allah will make him recount His blessings (i.e. the blessings which He had bestowed upon him) and he will recount them (and admit having enjoyed them in his life).

(Then) will Allah say: 'What did you do (to requite these blessings)?'

He will say, 'I fought for You until I died as a martyr.'

Allah will say, 'You have told a lie. You fought so that you might be called a brave warrior, and you were called so.' Then orders will be passed against him and he will be dragged with his face downward and cast into hell.

Then will be brought forward a man who acquired knowledge and imparted it (to others) and recited the Qur'an. He will be brought, and Allah will make him recount His blessings and he will recount them and admit having enjoyed them in his lifetime. Then will Allah ask, 'What did you do (to requite these blessings)?' He will say, 'I acquired knowledge and disseminated it and recited the Qur'an seeking Your pleasure.' Allah will say, 'You have told a lie. You acquired knowledge so that you might be called a scholar, and you recited the Qur'an so that it might be said, "He is a *Qāri*"' and such has been said.' Then orders will be passed against him and he shall be dragged with his face downward and cast into the Fire.

Then will be brought a man whom Allah had made abundantly rich and to whom He had granted every kind of wealth. He will be brought and Allah will make him recount His blessings and he will recount them and admit having enjoyed them in his lifetime.

Allah will (then) ask: 'What have you done (to requite these blessings)?'

He will say: 'I spent money in every cause in which You wished that it should be spent.'

Allah will say: 'You are lying. You did (so) that it might be said about (you): "He is a generous fellow" and so it was said.' Then will Allah pass orders and he will be dragged with his face downward and thrown into hell." (*Muslim*)

In Islam, certain deeds are very valuable and highly praised. Fighting for the religion of Allah, learning the Islamic disciplines and teaching them, and making donations to the poor are some such deeds. However, this hadith clearly teaches us that without sincerity, no actions are acceptable in the Divine Presence even though they might seem very valuable actions externally.

Sincerity towards Allah

Faith does not consist in mere words, but is demonstrated by the actions of the faithful. A faithful man or woman obeys the commandments of Allah with his/her whole heart and refrains from forbidden things without complaining. They prefer Allah over everything. Those who prefer worldly gains over Allah are the hypocrites. They use Islam as a cover for their mischief and deceive the believers. Such people accept their *nafs* as their supreme Lord. Allah says concerning such people:

Did you not see him who takes as his god his own vain desire? Allah has, knowing (him as such), left him astray, and sealed his hearing and his heart, and put a cover on his sight. Who, then, will guide him after Allah (has withdrawn guidance)? Will you not then receive admonition? (Jāthiyah, 45:23)

This verse teaches us that vain desires should be eliminated when a person serves Allah.

For the friends of Allah, sincerity has a very deep meaning. It means preferring Allah over everything else. Abū Yazīd al-Bistāmī once listened to the verse of the Qur'an: "Among you are some that hanker after this world and some that desire the hereafter" (Āl 'Imrān, 3:152). He started sobbing and said: "These words are the words of regret from Allah to us. He is saying that some choose the other world and some choose this world where are 'the people who choose only Me and My pleasure?'"

A little amount of worship which is done in sincerity is better than a great amount which lacks sincerity and good intention. The Prophet (upon him blessings and peace) says: "Perform your deeds in sincerity. (If you behave like this) even a small number of deeds are enough." He also said: "Allah does not look at your bodies and your wealth. He looks at your hearts (in order to see your sincerity) and deeds." In the following Qur'anic verse, Allah says that He created man in order to test the quality of his deeds: "He who has created death as well as life, so that He might put you to a test [and thus show] which of you is best in conduct, and [make you realize that] He alone is almighty, truly forgiving." (*Mulk*, 67:2) Of course the most significant characteristic of a righteous deed is the quality of the sincerity in which it was performed. Allah has different ways of testing the sincerity of man. Sometimes the believers are persecuted and tortured due to their faith and ideals. If they do not swerve and keep true to their faith, then they prove their sincerity and loyalty to Allah.

> *Alif Lām Mīm. Do men think that they will be left alone on saying, 'We believe', and that they will not be tested? We did test those before them, and Allah will certainly know those who are true from those who are false. ('Ankabūt, 29:1-3)*

However, we should not misunderstand the nature of sincerity, especially in refraining from performing good deeds due to the fear of ostentation. Sometimes Satan inspires man not to do a good action because he is not sincere, and in that way keeps man away from good actions. We might sometimes get the feeling of ostentation and lack of sincerity in our actions. However, instead of refraining from these good actions, we should strive to correct our intentions. The path of sincerity is not an easy path. There are many difficulties. It requires fighting against the *nafs* and its base desires. We can climb to the pinnacle of sincerity step by step. It is necessary that we both use our willpower and to ask for divine help in attaining this station. In order to achieve this aim, the following points should be followed:

Sincerity towards Allah

1) Through remembrance of Allah and the repetition of His names we must try to feel Allah's presence at all times. When we perform an action, we must know that Allah is watching over us.

2) We must keep a spiritual communication with the Prophet and other good people who follow the path of the Prophet (upon him blessings and peace). Through this spiritual connection we must strive to obtain their spiritual energy, which is called *fayd* in Sufi terminology.

3) We must attend the Islamic *suhbah*s (sermons and talks about Islam). In these gatherings we must try to enjoy the sweetness of brotherhood in Islam. We must also learn how to sacrifice ourselves for our brothers and sisters.

4) We should serve all humanity and love all people for the sake of Allah.

5) We should eat only what is earned by *halāl* (Islamically permitted) means. When the food comes from *harām* (illegal) ways, the heart cannot find any inclination towards serving Allah sincerely.

The important thing is that through these works we must realize the beauties of Islam in our hearts and attain the reality of sincerity in our deeds. It is very difficult nowadays to find sincere people. People are mostly running after worldly gains and they think of human beings as mere objects used to reach these targets. May Allah help us all in the path of attaining sincerity towards Him, the Almighty.

6.

Fear and Hope

"**W**ould You destroy us for the deeds of the foolish ones among us?" (*A'rāf*, 7:155)

A person's life moves in a course between fear and hope. It is necessary for a believer to maintain a balance between fear and hope through his or her entire life. For at the one extreme of fear there is despair, and at the opposite extreme is over-confidence and certainty. For this reason, being certain of Allah's forgiveness or abandoning hope of His generosity is forbidden in Islam. A perfect believer is one who maintains a balance between these two stances, as described in the Qur'an:

> *They forsake their beds and give up sleep, while they call on their Lord, in fear and hope; and they spend (in charity) out of the sustenance which We have bestowed on them. (Sajda, 32:16)*

Absolute despair or abandoning hope in Allah's compassion is a denial of His mercy, and ultimately means the denial of Allah's generosity, omnipotence and magnificence. However, the opposite attitude – absolute confidence in Allah's generosity – results in denial of Allah as *al-Qahhār* (the Subduer), and to a disregard of His recompense.

In short, a person must keep a balance without fearing Allah to the point of despair, but also without being hopeful to the point of neglecting one's duties. Extraordinary events, like the earthquake we recently experienced in Turkey (1999 earthquake which killed thousands of people), may make maintaining this balance very difficult at times.

A believer should be in such a state of mind that whenever he or she is told, "Only one person will be able to enter Paradise!" that person should ask themselves "Will it be me?" or whenever he or she is told "There is only one person that will enter Hell!" he or she should wonder "Will I be that person?"

Allah the Almighty warns people and teaches them through heavenly or earthly disasters to inculcate consciousness of the divine in their hearts, and to protect them from following their own desires. It is sheer folly to believe that these calamities happen by accident or at random. The death and injury of thousands of people and the resulting destitution and homelessness that these disasters cause are not meaningless or pointless. If this were the case, it would be impossible to understand the logical points of life, death and the divine program, and to explain them plausibly. These disasters are the manifestations of divine greatness, and the Creator's omnipotence. Rūmī said on this matter:

The world we live in is limited and mortal. The essential thing is the eternal and infinite world. Think so deeply that you will not curtain your heart from the eternal world with the pale miniatures, perishable shapes and dissolving fashions of this world! Although this world seems very important and vast to your eyes, think that it is not even a molecule in comparison to divine power. Watch out and look around at how an earthquake, a cyclone, or a flood devastates the world! (Mathnawī, Vol. I, 425)

We continuously watch how earthquakes and floods kill thousands of people all over the world every other day. Here are mass deaths that our Prophet (upon him blessings and peace) mentioned as a sign of the doomsday! In all these events there are countless lessons for us. Therefore, this disaster (1999 earthquake in Turkey that killed thousands of people) should be analyzed from a metaphysical perspective rather than be attributed to purely external causes. We should not fall into error when looking at the disaster from the point of a materialistic world philosophy instead of Islamic criteria. We should try to read the divine will behind all these disasters.

The universe – from the microscopic to the cosmos and the eternal world beyond – is programmed in detail according to a divine order. From the motion of the sun and other masses in space to that of the smallest parts of the atom and mysterious invisible rays, everything is moving in a course beyond our perception and imagination. Everything falls within this divine program. Even an unbeliever would not imagine that the speed of the sun quickens or slows down, or that a day on Earth lasts more than or less than twenty-four hours. Their hearts recognize and secretly admit the ultimate power of the divine will. However, caving to their desires, they interpret the basic laws of the divine order as "the laws of nature," assuming them a source of active power. Yet these laws and principles are the divine rules and practices (*ādāt Allāh*) which govern the universe.

This world is a world of causes. Allah, as the Causator of all causes *(musabbib al-asbāb)*, has tied everything to a certain cause. If the divine will manifested Itself without a cause, no one would endure the spiritul weight of this manifestation; also, there would be no justification for testing mankind's actions if the causation principle were not respected. Hence the people of divine

Fear and Hope

knowledge look at the Creator of causes and do not stop at the cause itself. Those who have no clue of the divine presence wander around ordinary causes, idly latching on purely physical explanations, such as blaming tectonic faults for earthquakes.

In order to discipline the unbelievers and the unjust, Allah turns "natural" incidents into material and moral torment. He turns the positive characteristics of natural elements like fire, water and wind into devastating powers. It is a kind of spiritual blindness not to see the divine will in the basis of events occurring in nature. Rūmī warns:

> *Do not forget that this world is like a piece of straw before the divine power. The divine will elevates it sometimes and lowers it at others, either leaving it strong or breaking it, bringing it to the right or to the left. It is sometimes rendered into a rose garden and sometimes into a bush.*

Allah wanted this world to be a testing ground. He shows His majesty (*jalāl*) alongside His beauty (*jamāl*) as two complementary things. The manifestation of Allah's kindness and beauty is realised through sincere prayers, alms, and pious deeds. But the manifestation of the wrath of Allah is brought about through forbidden practices and oppression. Apart from such causes, however, it also occurs in order to test people's patience and their submission to the divine will. Thus, Allah tests His servants in different ways. This is stated in the Qur'an: "Be sure We shall test you with something of fear and hunger, some loss in goods, lives and the fruits of your toil, but give glad tidings to those who patiently persevere" (*Baqara*, 2:155).

Even prophets, despite their innocence, have suffered severe ordeals and trials. The Prophet Job's (upon him blessings and peace) test was a very interesting one. Allah tested this prophet by first taking his property away from him. His sheep were destroyed in a flood and his crops laid waste with a strong wind. Then his children were all killed in an earthquake. After all of these trials, Allah sent a terrible disease to Job (upon him blessings and peace) who stayed steady and calm in complete trust in Allah. He did not complain about his disease, but submitted himself to Allah.

As a result of his great patience and submission, Allah the Almighty removed all of his diseases and troubles, and returned his family to him and a life that was even better than what it had been previously.

This example indicates that in some disasters innocent children may die, sincere and devout people may die; but through this disaster their sins may be forgiven. The Prophet Muhammad (upon him blessings and peace) said in this regard: "When Allah predestined a rank for a servant in His sight, and the person cannot reach this rank through his own deeds, Allah will send some trials and tribulations. Then He bestows patience upon His servant so that He can attain that rank!" "At the side of Allah, the servant has a rank that he or she cannot reach through worship alone. Until this position is reached, Allah sends to the servant things which he or she does not desire (calamities or troubles)." (*Musnad Abū Ya'lā, Sahih Ibn Hibbān*)

Moses (upon him blessings and peace) met a person on his way to Mount Sinai. The person said to Moses, upon him blessings and peace:

"O *Kalīm Allāh*! (he who speaks to Allah) I have a request: please pray for me on Mount Sinai!"

Moses (upon him blessings and peace) asked:

"What is your request? Tell me, so that I can ask it of Allah."

"O Messenger of Allah! This is a secret between Allah and me."

Then Moses (upon him blessings and peace) reached Sinai. He talked to Allah and beseeched Allah to grant that person his wish, and then Allah told him that his prayer had already been answered. On his return, Moses (upon him blessings and peace) stopped where he had met the man in order to tell him the good news, but he saw that wild animals had killed him. He was confused by what had happened, and he said:

"O my Lord! What secret is this? How did You accept his request?"

Allah said to him:

"O Moses! This servant asked of Me a spiritual rank to which he could not reach by his own efforts and deeds. So I gave him this affliction. Thus, I elevated him to the position he asked of Me."

Once the Prophet (upon him blessings and peace) stated: "Whenever Allah gives trouble to His servant, He either gives it in order to forgive his sin or to elevate him to an upper rank." (*Musnad Ahmad*)

Therefore the manifestation of Allah's enormous power should not lead to a sense of hopelessness; nor should Allah's kindness lead to an absolute confidence in one's goodness.

The divine natural laws (*sunnat Allāh*) and events such as earthquakes, fires, wars, plagues, droughts, and, on the other hand, Allah's mercy and blessings, are formed according to the servants' spiritual states. If most of the servants are on the right path, rain comes down as a mercy and a blessing, and happiness follows. However, if most of the community are inclined to their earthly desires, then floods, droughts or earthquakes become inevitable. These sad events occur because of sins or rebelliousness committed by people. In other words, natural disasters happen only after spiritual quakes already took place due to corrupt hearts. Allah states in the Qur'an: "Verily never will Allah change the condition of a people until they change what is in themselves." (*Ra'd*, 13:11)

Surely Allah is not an oppressor. It is a fact that these disasters occurred because of people's rebelliousness and oppression. It is inevitable that those who oppose the divine order and sacred principles will activate the divine revenge. Allah states in Quran: "…Not a leaf does fall but with His knowledge. There is not a grain in the darkness (or depths) of the earth, nor anything fresh or dry (green or withered), but is (inscribed) in a record clear (to those who can read)." (*An'ām*, 6:59) It would not be plausible to accept that the whole country has been shaken by itself when even a leaf does not fall without Allah's knowledge.

It cannot be denied that a disaster happens due to some physical reasons such as unstable foundations in buildings, inadequate rescue operations and so on. Likewise, it cannot be denied that people's spiritual states and their actions – good or evil – play a role in the triggering or the deflection of earthquakes. It is a great mistake to see only one side of the coin. Unfortunately, it is very disappointing to see some heedless people increase their rebellion against God rather than feeling remorse for their mistakes at the time of disasters. Rūmī says of this kind of people:

What a pity for those who instead of benefiting from the divine warnings as a remedy for their troubles make it a poison for themselves! It is because of this that Allah's

Fear and Hope

wrath increases the darkness in their eyes. They cannot see the hell waiting to destroy them! Woe betides them!

It is, of course, necessary to take every measure in preparation against possible future disasters. Then, after taking the necessary steps people should resign themselves to Allah. Once ʿUmar (may Allah be pleased with him) was passing quickly by a shaky wall which was about to collapse. His friends said, "O Commander of the Muslims! Are you trying to evade what Allah has ordained?" ʿUmar replied,"I take refuge from one destiny of Allah to another destiny of Allah."

Materialistic people exaggerate the power of taking such physical measures and think that "If buildings were strong enough, this earthquake would not have killed so many people." But when things are dependent on the divine will, the real cause overcomes all kinds of precautions and the divine will manifests itself at all costs. For example, an earthquake would occur at, say, 11.4 on the Richter scale instead of 7.4, or there could be another strong cause. The earthquake in Kobe is a very good example of this. There, houses were built with greater durance against earthquakes. Yet, unfortunately, at the time the earthquake struck, the gas pipes blew up and a sudden fire erupted; ultimately, six thousand people were killed in the ensuing blaze. A twenty-second earthquake was enough to destroy the wealth of all the people, which had taken years to accumulate.

Since we are the servants of Allah, we are obliged to take the necessary steps to prepare against future disasters. But it should be known that such measures are not a guarantee against our destiny. Measures give positive results only as far as they are in line with the divine destiny. The opposite behavior is the kind of behavior the tribe of Thamūd showed toward the people of ʿĀd.

The tribe of Thamūd had unwarily attributed the destruction of 'Ād to reasons other than Allah's wrath, which was due to their rebelliousness against Allah. They said: "The tribe of 'Ād was destroyed because they did not construct strong buildings, instead they built their houses on soft ground. We have built our houses on rocks, and so we will not suffer from any natural disaster." Indeed they had built very strong houses on high places by carving the rocks.

Nevertheless, the people of Thamūd were destroyed because they had gone astray. A terrible noise came from under the ground and destroyed them. Allah stated this in following verse: "The (mighty) blast overtook the wrong-doers, and they lay prostrate in their homes before the morning, as if they had never dwelt and flourished there. Behold! Thamūd rejected their Lord and Cherisher! Away with Thamūd!" (*Hûd*, 11:67-68)

It is evident that constructing strong buildings is not in itself a sufficient protection from natural disasters. All behavior that attracts Allah's anger such as dissension, ingratitude, rebellion and sin, leads to Allah's punishment. When the moral order in the land and the sea is violated, disasters occur one after another. This reality is stated in the Qur'an: "Mischief has appeared on the land and the sea because of what the hands of men have earned, so that Allah may give them a taste of some of their deeds, in order that they may turn back from evil." (*Rūm*, 30:41)

The punishment in the foregoing verse is described as only partial. It is implied that the main punishment will be in the thereafter. It is also stated that this punishment is only a warning. Therefore, one should take refuge in Allah more than before and ask forgiveness from Him. For Allah states: "Allah is not going to send them a chastisement while you were among them; nor was He going to send it while they asked for pardon" (*Anfāl*, 8:33).

Besides asking forgiveness and praying two *rak'ah*s (units of prayer), we should seek refuge in Allah's mercy and compassion as Allah states: "O you who believe! Seek help with patient perseverance and prayer; for Allah is with those who patiently persevere." (*Baqara*, 2:153)

Once the Prophet (upon him blessings and peace) said: "If anyone aids and consoles any victim of a disaster, Allah will reward him twice" (*Rāmūz al-Ahādīth*). We must remember that we could have been in that situation instead of them, and they could have been in our situation. Therefore, we should be charitable to them as a way of being grateful to Allah. We should reach out to help the destitute, injured, and saddened people living in a disaster area, and remedy their grief and pain as soon as we can.

We should also take the opportunity to increase our good deeds, as Rūmī said: "In such a case implore Allah! Cry unto Allah and praise Him, and increase your good deeds!"

We, in some sense, live a life which has been given back to us as a gift. In the wake of a terrible disaster which killed and injured thousands of people, we are the lucky people who were returned to this world once again and given extra time to increase our good deeds. As such, it will no longer be a valid excuse to say, "O our Lord! Send us back into the world so that we can devote our lives worshipping to You." Such a terrible event should therefore awaken us. Taking advantage of this opportunity, we should reorganise our lives by frequently reflecting upon death in the spirit of the saying "Die before death comes to you." We should train our hearts with patience, resignation, steadfastness and prayers in the tranquil state of submission to Allah.

The following Qur'anic verse, which discusses when the Prophet Moses (upon him blessings and peace) sought refuge in Allah when Mount Sinai was shaken by an earthquake, contains an important lesson for us:

And Moses chose seventy of his people for our place of meeting; when they were seized with violent quaking, he prayed, "O my Lord! If it had been Your will, You could have destroyed, long before, both them and me; would You destroy us for the deeds of the foolish ones among us? This is no more than Your trial: by it You cause whom You will to stray, and You lead whom You will into the right path. You are our protector; so forgive us and give us Your mercy; for You are the best of those who forgive. (A'rāf, 7:155)

Thus, we have seen that even prophets were not free from being tested; their hearts were tested with terrible calamities for their submission, appreciation, fear and love of Allah. In the end, they always maintained a state of fear and hope, and were the leaders of selected people who attained Allah's approval. All of us must live in accordance with Allah's sanction, maintaining a balance of fear and hope both in safety and hardship.

O Lord! Protect the Muslim community from calamity and suffering, and from Your wrath! Place us among those fortunate people who have attained Your divine favors by showing patience in a state of fear (from Your wrath) and hope (in Your mercy), in safety and in hardship! Bestow tranquillity and calmness upon our hearts! Transform these dark days of torment and trouble into blessed and happy mornings!

Amin!

7.
Heedlessness

A traveller who was travelling in a vast desert suddenly encountered a wild animal and took to his heels. But however fast he ran, he knew that the animal would catch up with him, so he jumped into a well without a second thought. As he was falling into the depths of the well he caught hold of a branch that jutted out from the wall. He grasped the branch with all his might for dear life. At the bottom of the well there were snakes ready to devour him. Then he saw two mice – one black and one white – gnawing at the root of the branch. He became so fearful that he almost fainted. The next moment he also saw a honeycomb in the wall and said to himself, "Let me taste this honey, I might not get another chance to find such sweet food."

And the man in peril became engrossed in the honey, forgetting his pitiful condition. He was like an ostrich who puts its head in the sand, thinking to hide itself. His eyes were blinded by the passing taste of the honey. Rather than trying to get out of the well, he enjoyed eating the honey while the mice ate up the root of the branch. The poor traveller fell down and was devoured.

In this story the well represents calamities and worldly life, the dragons and snakes represent evil characteristics, the honey worldly lusts, the white and black mice represent the passing days and nights, and the traveller represents us – the ordinary heedless man. The branch represents one's life-span: when it is eaten up by the mice of time, life ends. The entire story is a parable for the situation of mankind which was sent to this world for a mission but forgot its duy for the fleeting passions of the flesh.

Man's salvation lies in the cleansing of evil characteristics and using time in the best way. That is why man is created and given time – to realize himself.

Every creature on the face of the earth can only realize happiness by living their life in accordance with their true nature. Human beings, who are superior to all other creatures in this world, prosper only through understanding their *raison d'être* and arranging their life in accordance with the will of Allah. A life spent away from Allah, in ignorance of oneself and of one's true essence, is a life of misery. A person who lives in such a way is described as heedless (*ghāfil*). It is a delusion for a human being to be unaware of his true nature, his position, and the wisdom and purpose of his or her life and death. It is difficult to imagine an intelligent person who does not want to understand the real wisdom and secrets of a human being's arrival into this world from an invisible world, and then passing away after having been examined.

To understand the real meaning of humanity, life, and death is only attainable through avoidance of heedlessness. This, in turn, is possible only through sound reasoning and a spiritually developed heart. Natural human tendencies such as negligence, lust, arrogance, ambition, envy, extravagance, and anger are all the destructive manifestations of heedlessness. Being addicted to such traits and drowning in their whirlpools is the greatest delusion. It is because of this delusion and the human being's inclination to the *nafs* (lower self or ego) that sins block awareness

Heedlessness

of *haqīqah* (reality). They may damage a human being's honor, darken the spirit and lead to a disregard of the Creator. The Qur'an makes the following reference to such people: "Woe to those whose hearts are hardened against the remembrance of Allah!" (*Zumar*, 39:22).

Indeed, when morality weakens in one's heart, spiritual depth and true understanding will soon weaken also. Such a person will not realise *istiqāmah* (uprightness) anymore. Onw who indulges in sins becomes blind to his or her own faults. Heedless people under the influence of the *nafs* (ego) do not notice the damage that they have inflicted upon themselves, for they are blind and deaf to reality. Someone who has a wound in his finger can eat with this finger without feeling any dislike, whereas those who are at the same table with him cannot eat because of disgust at his wound. In the same way, heedless people will not feel the damage they inflict on others. They are engulfed in their heedlessness like a soldier in his armor. They are blind and deaf to reality and to all things Divine. Allah describes these people as "Deaf, dumb and blind..." (*Baqara*, 2:18)

Rūmī narrates the funny story of a heedless deaf man's visit to his neighbor for the latter's being sick. The deaf man did not visit his sick neighbor with a good intention, he only visited him to be seen by others. Similarly the sick man was also a heedless person, who at the first mistake of the visitor started accusing him without giving the benefit of doubt to the visitor. The story goes:

A wise friend of the deaf man said to him:

"Your neighbor is ill. Did not you know?"

Having heard this, the heedless man started calculating how to visit his neighbor:

"If I visit my neighbor, how would I be able to understand the ill man with my deaf ears?"

Then he said:

"When a person becomes sick his voice weakens. So I would not be able to understand any of his words."

However he decided to visit his neighbor anyway, thinking:

"I have no way except to visit him since he is my neighbor. Otherwise everybody will blame me for not visiting my neighbor and this will bring me much disrespect."

Then he made a plan:

"When I visit him I will try to understand what he says by looking at the movements of his lips. I will not show my neighbor that I cannot not hear him. Anyhow he will not be able to notice my deafness because of his own pain."

First I will say:

"How are you my dear neighbor?"

He will probably reply:

"I am well."

Then I will say:

"Praise be to Allah!"

Then I will ask:

"What have you eaten today?"

He will possibly say:

"I have had soup and juice."

Then I will say:

"I hope you enjoyed it!"

Heedlessness

Then I will ask:

"So which doctor is coming to examine you?"

He would say:

"So and so..."

And I will say nice words to him in order to boost his morale:

"You are a very lucky man. It is good that you called him. If he comes, everything will be fine."

The poor deaf man went to visit his neighbor after planning the whole dialogue, questions and answers in his mind.

First he asked as he planned:

"How are you my dear neighbor?"

His neighbor replied moaning in severe pain:

"I am in a very bad condition. It feels as if I am dying."

But since the deaf man did not hear the answer he immediately said:

"Thanks to Allah!"

The sick man was hurt by these words and deeply annoyed. He could not understand his neighbor's attitude. He thought to himself:

"My neighbor wants me dead!"

The deaf man asked his second question unwarily:

"What have you eaten?"

The annoyed neighbor replied in anger:

"Poison!"

Then the deaf said:

"I hope you enjoyed it!"

The sick man became angry – he was not a patient man. Then the deaf man said:

"Which doctors are coming to examine you?" The sick man's anger reached its peak. He shouted:

"Whom would you expect to come? The Angel of death, of course!"

But the deaf man could not hear what his neighbor told him and could not understand his attitude. Instead he replied:

"You are a very lucky man. This doctor brings health whereever he goes. You should be very happy for his coming!"

Then he left, feeling deep satisfaction his task was done. As he was leaving the house he thought to himself:

How fortunate that I visited my neighbor! I have safeguarded my reputation and brought some happiness to an unfortunate man."

Yet this stupid man's visit had actually been detrimental, even though he mistakenly thought that it had been profitable. The sick man now uttered harsh words about his neighbor:

"Now I have realized that our so-called neighbor was our mortal enemy! What a shame that I did not know this earlier!"

He was cursing his neighbor behind his back, saying:

"Visiting the sick is done for the sake of Allah and in order to console the sick. However, this man did not come for the sake of Allah, but for the sake of people. Nor did he come to inquire about my health but for enmity, and to offend me, and take revenge upon a sick man! He wanted to satisfy his bad heart by seeing his enemy in such a poor and weak position! However, I have never hurt him during the time that we have been neighbors"

Rūmī explains this story:

"The deaf person hurts someone else with the intention of pleasing him. He put his neighbor's heart into flames with his fictitious words. By visiting his sick friend in a hypocritical way, he has committed a sin."

"Because of his words based on guesses, their neighborliness and friendship was destroyed."

"On the other hand, the sick man was defeated by his anger and could not show patience. By acting in such a way, he was deprived of any divine reward. He did not try to learn the intention of this deaf neightbour. On the contrary, he did not show any good will towards him!"

Many people get caught in such situations. They worship and behave not solely for Allah's sake, but for their own interests. They try to gain Paradise by worship mixed with *nafs*."

"Their worship conceals sins and association of partners with Allah. To worship for someone else's sake is a grave sin. The prayer performed ostentatiously, though viewed as pure from the outside, soils the heart with the association of partners to Allah. Just as water loses its sweet taste with a single dirty drop, so too does worship performed with a sick and heedless heart." (Adapted from *Mathnawī*, V.I, 3360-95)

The deaf man's interpretation of his sick neighbour's behavior and his words according to his heedless understanding remind us of the moral deafness in today's people. The behavior of today's deaf vying for the closure of religious schools and Qur'an courses cannot be explained plausibly in any other way.[6] The behavior of heedless administrators, who are deaf to public protest to this new regulation, is the best example of heedlessness. Those who unconsciously benefit from the advantages of this world do actually try to be happy with fleeting favors. They consider their life in this world to be a Paradise. But it is absolutely true that those who loot these divine beauties will meet a severe reckoning in the hereafter.

Rūmī describes heedlessness, that is, the inclination of human nature to worldly affairs and bounties, in the following way:

"When you eat and drink the delicious foods of this world, you eat and drink as if in a dream. When you wake up, you feel hungry and thirsty again! The food you have consumed in your dream has brought you no benefit. The world is like a mere dream. The world and its favors are like someone who asks for something in his dream and it is granted to him. When he awakes, there is no sign of these favors he had received in his dream! This world is made of passing joys given in a dream."

Allah states in the Qur'an:

"Then did you not see such a one as takes as his god his own vain desire?" (Jāthiya, 45:23)

The "ears" in the story above may suppose themselves to understand words and letters. Again the "eyes" may suppose that they can see something. But what of the internal ears that are meant to hear hidden secrets and voices? And what of the internal eyes that are meant to observe divine secrets? The deafness of the

---

6. The author reminds us of the official closing down of religious high schools and the difficulties brought by new regulations to the learning of the Qur'an in Turkey in recent years.

Heedlessness

heart and the blindness of the eyes make a heedless person unfortunate both in this world and in the hereafter.

The Prophet Jonah (upon him blessings and peace) once said to Gabriel:

"Can you show me the person in this world who worships Allah the most?"

Gabriel showed him a person whose hands and feet were rotten from leprosy, and whose eyes had been lost. The man was saying:

"O Allah! It is no one but You that gave me whatever You gave through these hands and feet. And it is no one but You that save me from whatever You saved me from. O my God! You left only one desire deep in my heart: to reach You."

Once hearts beat only for the sake of Allah, intentions and behavior become very different from what they once were. Therefore, in order to escape from heedlessness, it is necessary to purify our hearts and cleanse our *nafs*, emptying our hearts of everything except the remembrance of Allah, and to watch for the manifestation of wisdom and grace in this universe.

For a person to do otherwise it would mean that they will not be able to save themselves from heedlessness, and they will lead themselves to a life of deprivation in this world and in the hereafter. We must be aware of our Creator and our *raison d'être* as much as we can, and we should bring ourselves to the Qur'an and Sunnah with a heart filled with contemplation and wisdom.

Human beings should live close to their Creator. They should worship Allah, Who has given them all of His favors during their lives, has forgiven their sins, and knows all their secrets. Worship is limited to only a short time, but faith and service are for life.

May Allah include us among His friends who are on the right path and have a heart filled with awareness of the truth!

Amin!

8.

The beautification of death

"Beautification of death" denotes a level of maturity where one can neutralize the negative and unattractive aspects of the lower self (*nafs*), elevating an ordinary person to the level of a perfect human being as recommended in the rule "Die before death comes to you."

With such maturity one comes closer to the Creator and all carnal desires lose their sway. A person can enjoy happiness in his or her worship, kindness in dealings with people, and virtue in manners. The soul begins to enjoy the pleasure of getting closer to one's Lord. That is why Rūmī says about the time before he experienced the state of nearness to Allah: "I was immature," about the period of obtaining divine pleasure: "I became ripe," and about the period of in which the mysteries of the universe unfolded to him like a book: "I was burned."

These expressions are the manifestation of the efforts in the way to Allah. Although the ways that lead to Allah are "as many as the number of the breaths of all creatures", the most effective one is the way of *faqr-u fanā'*. *Faqr-u fanā'* means to remove the ego and *mā siwā* – "everything but God" – from heart and soul, as a result of divine love. This results in the beautification of death, which turns into an eternal union with Allah as the manifestation of the saying mentioned above, and annihilation (*fanā'*) in Allah.

To attaining this prized manifestation is only possible if one observes the following conditions, which are valid for everybody:

a) *Tawbah* (repentance)

Sins are motivated by ignorance, sexual desire, arrogance, anger, hatred, blind ambition, jealousy and extravagance. These tendencies are obstacles which take man away from his Creator. If man becomes truly aware of himself, he can be disturbed by the weight of his vice. The hidden emotion of virtue awakes in his heart, and his heart finds peace in Allah by shedding tears of great regret and sorrow. This sorrow and regret is *tawbah* (repentance), which means literally turning to Allah voluntarily before the involuntary return of death comes. In other words, *tawbah* means removing the obstacles between man and Allah through the emotion of regret.

Tawbah is the first step which is necessary for the return to Allah, because sins are obstacles which decrease the sensitivity of the heart and slow it down. This state is just like cloudy images in a dirty mirror. In order to see the reflection in this dirty mirror properly it is necessary to wipe it with a clean cloth. Likewise, returning to Allah makes it necessary to cleanse the heart with *tawbah* from all sins, which are dross over the heart. That is why in all branches of *tasawwuf* the first thing to do is to ask Allah for forgiveness (*istighfār*). This looks just like the subtle point "*lā*" in the declaration of Oneness (*kalimat al-tawhīd*), *lā ilāha illā Allāh*, which means "There is no god but Allah." In other words, first it is necessary to remove all negatives and prepare a suitable base for the real objective.

Thus, seeking forgiveness from Allah is almost a requirement for sincere prayers. Rūmī says; "Seek forgiveness from Allah with a heart full of regret and tearful eyes because flowers bloom in moist soils."

b) *Zuhd* (asceticism)

Zuhd means freeing the heart from the grip of worldly luxuries, pleasures, property and position. In fact, death wipes out all of these in a moment. The essence of *zuhd* is to be able to give up life and property voluntarily before involuntary death comes. Human comprehension, between the two momentous realities of birth and death, cannot escape from the world of shadows and proceeds to the world of reality unless it reaches the real understanding of this world and the hereafter, modifying one's behavior accordingly. A wise man described this world, which exemplifies of divine wisdom, as *sayr-i bedāyī* for wise ones or "learning a lesson" from the ultimate secrets of Allah, and as "eating and passion" for the fool. If a person cannot put a limit to worldly desires in his or her heart, the consequence is frustration, which leads to destruction.

c) *Tawakkul* (reliance upon Allah)

Tawakkul means that a servant seeks refuge in his Lord and surrenders himself to Him before death comes. Trust in and submission to Allah's will does not mean one leaves all causes aside, but it means one realizes that if causes are not in accordance with the will of Allah, all efforts will be futile. Death is the true understanding of cause and fate relationship. Allah says: "If anyone puts his trust in Allah, sufficient is (Allah) for him."(*Talāq*, 65:3)

In other words, for the one whose heart is full of love for Allah, *tawakkul* means to trust in and submit only to Allah. Allah asked Moses about the staff in his hand and told him: "Cast it off!" for the rod impeded his true trust in Allah by giving him self-confidence. Again Allah says: "Put your trust in Allah if you have faith." (*Mā'idah*; 5: 23)

Tawakkul is not ignorance of precautions and efforts; on the contrary, it is submission to Allah's power only after one has taken such steps.

As a result of the Prophet Abraham's *tawakkul* and his submission to Allah the fire did not burn him. When he showed his true *tawakkul*, Allah ordered the fire to "be cool and secure for him!" For, as we said, *tawakkul* means the choice of submitting everything to Allah willingly before death comes. Rūmī, questioning our ordinary *tawakkul* and submission says: "Check yourself to see whether you have Abraham's quality or not. The fire recognizes and will not burn only those who properly submit themselves to Allah like Abraham."

d) *Qanāʿah* (contentment)

Qanāʿah means to desire no more than what is necessary. A compulsory contentment will come with death. The only cure for jealousy and blind ambition – the most dangerous of character traits – is to acquire the spirit of contentment, because the divine treasures contentment gives to the heart never end. The Prophet (upon him blessings and peace) is reported to have said: "Contentment is a treasure that is never exhausted." (Bayhaqi, *al-Zuhd al-Kabir*)

Therefore, the real measure of richness is contentment and satisfaction with the divine allotment. *Qanāʿah* means not to be jealous of those who have more. The pleasure of being rich-hearted can only be tested with contentment.

It is a principle of faith that sustenance is predetermined by the divine apportionment. When this is taken into consideration, it is obvious that blind ambition and covetousness are not only ugly but unreasonable. Yet, some people still cannot give up their blind ambition to become wealthy, although they witness that those who profit and those who consume are usually different people. Such people suffer from terminal egotism. To them wealth means power for themselves as well as for others. Quite often the admiration and attention that they derive from jealous people give them great pleasure.

Contentment is the only divine medicine that can cure all these illnesses. Only with the power of contentment is it possible to be free from the calamities a person can face from possessing great wealth. Contentment should not concern wealth only, but also the attention and admiration that emerge from the power that comes with wealth.

In brief, it is necessary for a person to understand that wealth belongs to Allah, and that man is just like a cashier. The caliph 'Alī (may Allah be pleased with him) says for those who do not remember death: "Most of the people try to accumulate wealth in order to make their inheritors fight."

f) *'Uzlah* (isolation or seclusion):

'Uzlah is a requirement in Sufi training to achieve the highest state. However, seclusion is not meant to cancel all social interaction. For common people, seclusion can be achieved by realizing seclusion internally among the crowds. It consists in isolating the heart from worldly affairs and direct one's attention toward Allah.

Yet, some saints practice *'uzlah* as actual isolation; however this does not hamper social life due to the small number of these people. Such isolation is in special cases. In general terms, *'uzlah* in religious training does not mean withdrawal from public life. On the contrary, it means isolation while being in public; in other words, being alone with Allah even in a crowd of people. It is being together with Allah in divine manifestations, before retiring into a grave, by leaving out all worldly relations. In short, it is being with Allah voluntarily; whereas death is an involuntary *'uzlah*.

f) *Dhikr* (remembrance):

Manifestations of divine effusion (*fayd*) are based on *mahabbah* (divine love). *Mahabbah* can be achieved to the extent of the place *dhikr* holds in the heart and mind. For love to take root in the heart and the mind is possible only by remembering the beloved; the more we remember Allah, the more we love Him.

As a source of divine effusion, *Lafza-i Jalāl* ("Allah") is the most effective one among the names of Allah. Because of its strength, it is advised for a devotee (*sālik*) to continue repeating *Lafza-i Jalāl* after a period of *istighfār* (repentance). Remembrance of Allah conduces to advancement in love of Allah (*mahabbat Allāh*) in proportion with its quantity and quality. In other words, the more *dhikr* is said and the more sincere it is, the greater manifestations will be attained.

With the taking root of remembrance of Allah in the heart, the manifestation of the believers's servanthood gets nearer to perfection. The Qur'an says: "In the remembrance of Allah do hearts find satisfaction." (*Ra'd*, 13:28)

If the *Lafza-i Jalāl* cannot settle in the heart, man remains trapped by material wealth and carnal desires. Another Qur'anic verse says: "Did you not see such a one as takes for his god his own passion (or impulse)? Could you be a disposer of affairs for him?" (*Furqān*, 25:43)

Morality, good deeds and spiritual manners settle in the hearts that are full of spirituality. Man gains the quality of being the most beautiful creature. On the other hand, *kufr* (infidelity),

The beautification of death

shirk (polytheism), bad deeds, passion and skepticism settle in the hearts that are full of sensuality. Then they start to control the heart: it becomes blind against the objective of creation. Sometimes its possessor even becomes inferior to other species!

The poet Nizāmī describes the end of those who were controlled by their *nafs* thus: "The pleasures of the world are like scratching an itchy palm. At first, scratching feels good, but it ends up hurting the palm." By expressing the importance of spiritual life al-Junayd al-Baghdādī describes the manifestation of the "beautification of death" and the command to "Die before death comes" as "Allah's taking your self from yourself then resurrecting you with Himself."

g) *Tawajjuh* (inclination)

Tawajjuh is to ignore all attractive calls except Allah's call. Death is the realization of this state. In reality a pious person cannot have any desire, friend and objective other than Allah. Even for a fleeting moment one cannot be heedless (*ghāfil*) of His presence. When death comes, one who is heedless of His presence will very unwillingly be taken away from everything he is inclined to other than Allah. Real happiness is to submit and turn to Allah and His consent while one is still alive.

h) *Sabr* (patience)

Sabr is to submit oneself to Allah by struggling quietly amid events that are undesirable and painful, without changing the balance between inner and outer qualities. The grave will be a place of compulsory patience away from all worldly desires. When we face events that require patience, it is necessary to use some moral qualities such as forgiveness, gentleness, humility, chastity, satisfaction, compassion, mercy, kindness and tolerance. It is very important that we be patient with everything that keeps man away from Allah's consent. The Qur'an commands us: "and be patient and constant, till Allah, do decide: for He is the best to decide." (*Yūnus*, 10:109)

Patience is a great armor against difficulties. Death is the end of diehard carnal desires, and the grave is the compulsory place of patience until the day of resurrection.

i) *Murāqaba* (contemplation)

Murāqaba means to leave one's power and strength aside. Death denotes the complete realization of this state. More precisely, *murāqaba* is to stay away from sins by feeling that one is under the divine observation all the time. Nothing in all of creation is out of His disposal.

Nothing can escape from death and resurrection. Existence and nonexistence, death and life, mortality and immortality are always interrelated. Every moment, thousands of cells die in the human body and thousands of them are recreated. Every moment, thousands of babies are born, and thousands of people die. Every moment, while lots of heedless people are enraptured by worldly pleasures, lots of pious people are in a state of supplication, seeking refuge with Allah. The grave – the last stop of the world – is waiting for everybody. All over the world there is only His disposition, sovereignty and divine arrangement. In order to enhance the attribute of servanthood in oneself, it is important to be aware of this divine observation before one dies. With imagination and thought, man can direct himself toward Allah, as it is stated in the wise saying: *"Whoever knows himself knows Allah."*

j) *Ridā* (contentment)

Ridā means living with the contentment of Allah by leaving out one's self-approval. Death means the realization of this state.

The beautification of death

Ridā is the maturation of comprehension through a process of purification of the heart and self. Man submits himself to Allah by escaping from the captivity of transitory and delusory things. With great spiritual happiness, a person realizes the fineness described in the expression below:

> *Whatever comes from You is fine with me*
>
> *Whether it is a budding rose or thorn*
>
> *Whether it is a robe of honor or a shroud.*
>
> *Your grace and Your wrath; both are fine!*

k)- *Tafakkur-i mawt* (reflecting on death):

The world is a school of faith in the fact that death is a law of obligatory transition. Rūmī says: "Die in order to resurrect." Reviving the heart is only possible if one gives up sensuality. The Prophet (upon him blessings and peace) says: "Remember the destroyer of pleasures often – death." (*Nasa'i, Tirmidhi, Ibn Majah*)

Taffakur-i mawt is to remember death voluntarily before it comes to you against your will. Thus, it is to be ready for the presence of Allah by abandoning sensuality. This is contemplation and consciousness based on faith (*īmān*).

Worldly desires, transitory hopes and consolations are like tree leaves falling on top of the graves. Every gravestone is a fiery advisor speaking with eloquent silence about death. The reason for building cemeteries inside cities, near roads, and in mosque courtyards is, in a way, to facilitate the contemplation of death.

Words cannot fully capture the frightening weight of death. All of a person's powers end when death comes. In the presence of death, the only response that comes from the world is tears and helpless sadness.

If man gives up sensual attributes voluntarily, Allah will certainly recreate him with His kindness and grace. In fact, Allah Most High says: "Can he who was dead, to whom We gave life and a light whereby he can walk among men, be like him who is in the depths of darkness, from which he can never come out? Thus, to those without Faith, do their own deeds seem pleasing."(*Anām*, 6:122)

The true servant joins those whose hearts are recreated, for he gives up the sensual pleasures of this world. The Prophet (upon him blessings and peace) said: "Be careful of the discernment (*firāsah*) of the believer, as he sees with the *nūr* (light) of Allah." (*Tirmidhi*)

All the above-mentioned expressions are the conditions that have to be practiced in one's spiritual life in order to fulfill the advice to "Die before death comes to you." The believers who are trying to follow these commands progress to the extent of the seriousness of their efforts and their steadfastness on the path. A sincere effort yields happiness with the help of divine support.

The world is a deceptive mirage and the hereafter is everlasting life. Death is the personal Judgment Day of a person. Let us wake up before our own reckoning so that we not become regretful. It is an unavoidable fact that every transitory creature is going to meet the Angel of death at an undisclosed place and time. There is no place where we can flee from death. Mankind just has to accept Allah's compassion and mercy as the only shelter by benefiting from the meaning of the verse "Therefore flee unto Allah [from all that is false and evil]" (*Dhāriyāt*, 51:50).

If a man lives under the commands of a carnal mind as if he only believed in this world, the grave is to him a dark corridor. The terror of death makes him feel such a pain that he cannot compare it with anything else. Yet if he applies the principles

The beautification of death

mentioned above, going beyond his worldly self and proceeding toward his angelic side hidden within, then death would be seen as a condition of communion with Allah. Thus, death, which causes shivers in most people, is transformed into eagerness of union with "the highest friend" (*al-rafīq al-aʿlā*). This kind of death is like "Shab-i ʿArūs," the wedding night as expressed by Rūmī, one of the greatest Sufis. Death has transformed from a terrible reality into something beautiful. The only way for such "beautification of death" is to increase in spirituality by following the conditions we have described. The best way is expressed in the verse "And serve your Lord until there comes to you the hour that is certain." (*Hijr*, 15:99) That is, be a proper servant to Him to the last breath. How happy are the ones who can return to their Lord before death comes!

O our Lord, let us wake up to the real world by catching the essence of "Die before death comes to you," and behold the universe with consciousness.

Amin!

9.

Rizq (sustenance)

Abu Hāzim said: "*I found the whole world in two things: the first is my sustenance and the second is the sustenance of another person. My sustenance will catch me even if I rode the wind and flew away. And if I tried to take someone else's sustenance, even if I rode the wind after it, I would never be able to catch it.*"

Deprivation, poverty, and not being able to find any livelihood or sustenance are some of the fears that burden the minds of human beings, often causing them great anxiety. Sustenance (*rizq*) constitutes a central point in the program of one's fate. It starts from the stage of human formation in the mother's womb, and continues until the time of death in accordance with one's destiny. The time of death is, in a sense, the point at which our acquisition of sustenance ends.

All creatures' sustenance has been predetermined; it neither increases nor decreases from what has been ordained. Holding fast to the means of earning sustenance (*tawassul bil-asbāb*) produces results only if such has been foreordained by Allah. The following verse states this very clearly:

وَمَا مِن دَآبَّةٍ فِي الْأَرْضِ إِلَّا عَلَى اللَّهِ رِزْقُهَا وَيَعْلَمُ مُسْتَقَرَّهَا وَمُسْتَوْدَعَهَا كُلٌّ فِي كِتَابٍ مُّبِينٍ

"There is no moving creature on earth but its sustenance dependent on Allah." (*Hūd*, 11:6)

Rizq (sustenance)

Allah grants every individual creature's share of sustenance. Because of that the friends of Allah hear expressions of gratitude for the blessings of Allah even in the songs of nightingales on rosewood trees. The following verse states how Allah Almighty provides even the sustenance of the wounded and disabled, and those who cannot properly obtain their own sustenance:

وَكَأَيِّنْ مِنْ دَابَّةٍ لَا تَحْمِلُ رِزْقَهَا اللَّهُ يَرْزُقُهَا وَإِيَّاكُمْ وَهُوَ السَّمِيعُ الْعَلِيمُ

"How many are the creatures that carry not their own sustenance? It is Allah who feeds (both) them and you: For He hears and knows (all things)." (*'Ankabūt*, 29:60)

It is also important to be aware of the diversity in the distribution of sustenance in the world. This diversity creates order and harmony in society rather than causing division and conflict. The Qur'an demonstrates that all worldly possessions ultimately belong to Allah and that they are distributed in accordance with the divine knowledge we call foreordained destiny (*qada'* and *qadar*).

Believers should believe that any diversity in the distribution of sustenance is in their favor. If the order of life were left to the weak device of human beings, whose perception is warped by their desires, ambitions and limitations, it would create anarchy in the universe. Allah states in the Qur'an:

أَهُمْ يَقْسِمُونَ رَحْمَةَ رَبِّكَ نَحْنُ قَسَمْنَا بَيْنَهُمْ مَعِيشَتَهُمْ فِي الْحَيَاةِ الدُّنْيَا وَرَفَعْنَا بَعْضَهُمْ فَوْقَ بَعْضٍ دَرَجَاتٍ لِيَتَّخِذَ بَعْضُهُمْ بَعْضًا سُخْرِيًّا وَرَحْمَتُ رَبِّكَ خَيْرٌ مِمَّا يَجْمَعُونَ

"Is it they who would portion out the mercy of your Lord? It is We Who portion out between them their livelihood in the life of this world: And We raise some of them above others in ranks, so that some may command work from others. But the mercy of your Lord is better than the (wealth) which they amass." (*Zukhruf*, 43:32)

The distribution of sustenance among creatures in this universe is one of the signs of Allah's sovereignty and power. At any time of the day, dining tables are well prepared for the creatures flying in the air, walking on land, or swimming in the sea. Moreover, generally, one being can notnourish itself with the food created for another being. In other words, the food for all creatures is diversified depending on their different environments and needs. This division of sustenance – as unlimited as the number of creatures in the universe, each fed differently one by one! – is the ultimate manifestation of wisdom, power, and sovereignty. Similarly, it is stated in another verse in the Qur'an:

أَوَلَمْ يَعْلَمُوا أَنَّ اللَّهَ يَبْسُطُ الرِّزْقَ لِمَن يَشَاءُ وَيَقْدِرُ إِنَّ فِي ذَٰلِكَ لَآيَاتٍ لِّقَوْمٍ يُؤْمِنُونَ

"Know they not that Allah enlarges provision or restricts it for any He pleases? Verily, in this are signs for those who believe!" (*Zumar*, 39:52)

The Messenger of Allah (upon him blessings and peace) says in this respect: "Whenever one of you looks at someone above their station, let them also look at someone below their station. This is necessary for you in order that you not to look down on the favors of Allah." (*Bukhārī, Muslim, Tirmidhī*)

Therefore the happiness and delight of our lives depend upon the belief that the share that was provided for us is best for us. There are so many events that appear to be misfortune at first sight, but their outcomes are really good fortune, just like poverty leading to Paradise. Likewise, there are so many events that

Rizq (sustenance)

appear to be good fortune at first, but their results are sad disappointment, such as wealth not spent in charity but instead upon cheap desires. Allah states:

$$\text{كُلُوا مِن طَيِّبَاتِ مَا رَزَقْنَاكُمْ وَلَا تَطْغَوْا فِيهِ فَيَحِلَّ عَلَيْكُمْ غَضَبِي وَمَن يَحْلِلْ عَلَيْهِ غَضَبِي فَقَدْ هَوَى}$$

> "Eat of the good things We have provided for your sustenance, but commit no excess therein, lest My wrath should descend on you: and those on whom My wrath descends do perish!" (*Ta-Ha*, 20:81)

In the light of all these truths, the believer's submission to Allah's distribution of sustenance is a way for his or her eternal happiness. Since sustenance was divided by the Creator before the human being was created, man should be in complete resignation to Allah so that he is able to enjoy the sustenance predestined for him and feel the taste of believing in destiny. It is stated in a hadith qudsī:

> *Allah, the Almighty, has commanded his angels in charge of the division of sustenance that: "If you find a servant of Mine who has completely focussed his or her concern on the hereafter, guarantee for that person the favors of heaven and earth! When you find a servant of Mine looking for his or her sustenance with fairness (without leaving the straight path) behave well with him and make his path easy!"* (Nawadir al-Usul)

This hadith explicitly shows that when a servant focuses his or her desires and intentions only to Allah, obeys His commands, worships Him only for His sake, and becomes a sincere and devoted believer, he/she is guaranteed the blessings of heaven and earth. Allah Almighty generously creates the reasons by which they will obtain their sustenance. This fact is stated in the following verse:

وَمَن يَتَّقِ اللَّهَ يَجْعَل لَّهُ مَخْرَجًا وَيَرْزُقْهُ مِنْ حَيْثُ لَا يَحْتَسِبُ

"And for those who fear Allah, He (ever) prepares a way out, and He provides for him from (sources) he never could expect." (*Talāq*, 65:2-3)

In addition, the Prophet (upon him blessings and peace) states: "If you put your faith exclusively in Allah, He will bestow on you your sustenance in the same way He provides for the birds. They go out in the morning with their stomachs empty and return filled in the evening. (*Tirmidhī, Ibn Mājah*)

Species like ants, which stock food in the summer for the winter, are very rare. It is a known fact that other animals, although they do not prepare for winter like an ant does, can survive the severe conditions of winter and reach spring safe and sound. How can the Creator forget His creations' sustenance in this perfect divine order which was established under His divinity and sovereignty?! However, laziness, stinginess, envy, not wanting to have children, etc. are wrong and blameworthy behavior regarding our sustenance in this world.

As stated above, Islam teaches that everybody's share of sustenance is predetermined, neither increasing nor decreasing at any point in time. Allah, Who created everything that exists, has granted every creature a living term and determined a sufficient amount of sustenance for this period. The life of a human, every breath taken and every single morsel consumed, is completely fixed within the panel of destiny and encoded in

Rizq (sustenance)

Adam's (upon him blessings and peace) descendants (*dhurriyyah*). But working to obtain the necessary allotted sustenance is also commanded upon the believers. Therefore, obeying the divine commands and working for sustenance are among our obligations. In other words, the distribution of pre-determined sustenance had been tied to the precondition of our labor. "Take the necessary measures, so do not then falsely blame predestination," says a famous Turkish proverb. Allah Almighty has equipped us with divine faculties such as willpower, entrepreneurship, responsibility, resignation and discernment. Ignoring these rules is in fact a form of rebellion against Allah.

Protecting ourselves from danger is inherent in our nature, such as when we consult a doctor and take medicine when ill, or flee from a dangerous fire or earthquake. Striving to obtain one's sustenance is a divine command in order to be protected from dangers. It is not incongruent with the belief in predestination. If it were, there would be no point in requiring servants to seek their sustenance. Disregarding the rules of causes is a revolt against Allah and a great sin. It is stated in the Qur'an:

وَأَن لَّيْسَ لِلْإِنسَانِ إِلَّا مَا سَعَىٰ

"Man can have nothing but what he strives for." (*Najm*, 53:39)

The Prophet (upon him blessings and peace) said. "For a man to take his rope and go into the forest to collect wood is better than to beg from people, whether or not people give him what he wants." (*Bukhārī*)

According to Ibn al-Firāsī's report, one day his father asked the Prophet (upon him blessings and peace) "Messenger of Allah!

Shall I ask from people what I need?" The Prophet (upon him blessings and peace) replied: "Do not ask anyone! However if you must, then ask from righteous people!" (*Nasa'i, Abu Dawud, Ibn Majah*)

Beside what we mentioned, Allah Almighty has appointed His creatures to be means for each other to acquire their sustenance. Looking after poor people, taking care of their needs and giving them part of what Allah has bestowed upon us is therefore great virtue and kindness. It is related that Gabriel (upon him peace) said, "If I had been from this world's community I would have loved these three things most: Guiding those who lost their way, loving those who worship in poverty, and helping poor people who have to look after many children."

Lawful food

Another important here is *halāl* (lawful) food obtained in legitimate ways – one of the greatest factors leading to one's perfection.

Once Sahl b. Tustarī sold a sheep to a man. After a while the man brought the sheep back to Tustarī and said:

"I want you to take this sheep back, because it does not eat grass."

Tustarī replied: "How do you know that?"

"I took her to a field to graze. She did not even have a single bit."

Tustarī replied:

"My friend! You must have done the wrong thing. It is not our animal's habit to eat something that belongs to somebody else. Go and give her the fodder that you own."

The man did as he was told and the sheep started to eat.

The Muslims' sensitivity about gaining *halāl* food was even affecting their animals once.

Choosing *halāl* sustenance means the light of life, the joy of the heart, and the essence of worship. It is one of the leading factors in achieving a sound heart. *Harām* (unlawful) sustenance, however, is a poison which destroys one's life, fire and disappointment of the heart. Humiliation in this world and in the hereafter, dishonor and calamity are all the terrible consequences of obtaining sustenance by illicit means.

Halāl possession and *halāl* nutrition are the means to reach Allah's approval while unlawful gain and food are causes of great regret and disappointment for those who use them. When property and children obsess one's heart, instead of it being reserved for Allah, the only result is sadness and despair. *Rūmī* explains this through the following example: "The water inside the ship sinks the ship. However, the water under the ship lifts it up. Because Solomon threw the love of worldly possessions out of his heart, he said 'I am poor, and it behooves a poor man to be with the poor!' and he reached a sublime position."

Allah states in the Qur'an:

$$\text{يَا أَيُّهَا النَّاسُ أَنْتُمُ الْفُقَرَاءُ إِلَى اللَّهِ وَاللَّهُ هُوَ الْغَنِيُّ الْحَمِيدُ}$$

"O men! It is you that have need of Allah: but Allah is the One free of all wants, worthy of all praise." (*Fātir*, 35:15)

That is why the Prophet (upon him blessings and peace) said about the belongings possessed only for the sake of religion and for Allah: "What a nice property it is which is spent for good!"

'Umar b. Khattāb (may Allah be pleased with him) said the following prayer: "O Allah! Entrust abundant property to our benevolent people! It is hoped that they will help those in need among us."

On the other hand, neither *zakāh* nor *sadaqah* (obligatory and voluntary charity) can originate in unlawful gain since it is not lawful property. Unlawful gain is a disgrace both in this world and in the hereafter. A lawful morsel fuels wisdom, learning and *ma'rifah* or knowledge in the body, and arouses love of Allah and ardor in the heart.

Just as it is impossibile to harvest barley from a field where only wheat was sown, it is impossible to achieve spiritual perfection with a body fed with illicit nutrition. If the body is not nourished with *halāl* food, which gives human beings the power to know Allah, spiritual perfection in the heart and humility in worship are not attainable.

Contemplate the following hadith qudsi: "I feel ashamed to call to account those who refrained from *harām* food."

It is therefore necessary to obtain sustenance by lawful means in this world. Only *halāl* food contains the power that keeps people on the straight path, equips them with divine wisdom, and guides them from the prison of the world to the light of Allah.

It should also be noted that there is a gray area in between the lawful and the unlawful. One needs to steer clear of it just as one would from the unlawful. Suspicious matters are like the private pasture of Allah, and whoever goes into that pasture will perish. The Messenger of Allah (upon him blessings and peace) said:

Rizq (sustenance)

Both lawful and unlawful things are evident, but in between there are dubious matters of which most people have no knowledge. Whosoever saves himself from these dubious matters saves his religion and honor. And whoever indulges in these dubious matters falls into the unlawful. He/she is like a shepherd who grazes his flock near the private pasture of someone else and at any moment they are liable to enter it. Beware! Every king has a private pasture and the private pasture of Allah on earth is what He has declared illicit.

Rūmī draws attention to the fact that licit food fills people with spirituality (*rūhaniyyah*) and divine light (*nūraniyyah*):

There is no food for the human being other than divine light. The spirit cannot be nourished by any other means.

Little by little restrain yourself from the foods and drinks of this world! These are not the actual nutriments of a human being.

Try to gain competence in obtaining the nutriments of heaven! Prepare yourself for the morsel of divine light!

Heed the command of the Qur'an: "Seek the bounty of Allah!" (Jum'a, 62:10)!

Beware lest the body not incline and submit, but instead become obdurate against Haqq (Truth) unless it feels hungry. Trying to subdue it while it is full is like trying to forge cold iron.

The nafs (lower self) resembles Pharaoh, who begged Moses (upon him blessings and peace) in the years of famine.

If you stay away from these crumbs, you will attain sublime and gracious sustenance.

Even if you eat tons of such spiritual food you will still walk as light as a feather.

Even if you eat from spiritual food as much as an ocean, you will still float like a ship.

The appetite of the stomach guides human to the hayloft, but the appetite of the heart guides human beings to fields of sweet basil.

An animal nourished with straw and barley ultimately becomes a sacrifice; those who are nourished with the light of haqq (truth) become a living Quran.

Give up your stomach and walk towards heart so that the peace of Allah comes to you!

Be aware that hunger is the basis of all remedies. Assimilate hunger with determination – do not scorn it!

Our expenses in this world are for the livelihood of our families and ourselves. However we must shun extravagance. Wealth and opportunities in this world are limited. They are entrusted to us by Allah, and we will be questioned about them in the hereafter. Spending them boorishly and thoughtlessly like today's capitalist societies endangers the lives of future generations. Among all animals, only human beings do not easily become satisfied. A wild animal attacks a flock of sheep only to quell its hunger at that moment. It does not continue killing afterwards thinking that "it will eat it the next day!" It veritably becomes a friend of the other sheep in the herd. On the contrary, human beings have limitless desires. The first condition to save a

Rizq (sustenance)

person from his or her endless ambitions is to protect it from extravagace by inculcating it the firm belief that sustenance neither increases nor decreases. The Qur'an states:

$$وَإِن مِّن شَيْءٍ إِلَّا عِندَنَا خَزَائِنُهُ وَمَا نُنَزِّلُهُ إِلَّا بِقَدَرٍ مَّعْلُومٍ$$

"And there is not a thing but its inexhaustible sources and treasures are with Us; but We only send down thereof in due and appointed measures." (*Hijr*, 15:21)

In this verse, it is explained that the division of sustenance is by divine will, and that ambition and greed are shut off from the intelligent person. The verse also states that sustenance is distributed by Allah. If we add up our new wishes and growing aspirations one after the other, this chain of desires are called worldly ambitions (*tūl-i amal*). These will only last until we reach the grave. Their consequences are disappointment and severe remorse. Worldly ambitions consist of limitless finite desires just like a shadow which disappears with the setting sun.

Sins darken the heart and make it deaf to reality: they desensitize the heart to the divine truth. In this respect, one of the causes of the illnesses of the heart is the consumption of unlawful foods. It has been narrated that the prayers of a person who ate illicit food will not be answered for forty days. The reason is that the circulation of a nutriment in the body takes forty days to complete. The above-mentioned report illustrates the ill effects of unlawful food on the spiritual well-being of the heart.

Thus, nourishment by unlawful means is a spiritual poison for the body. It is impossible to feel the good taste of worship in that state.

We should be alert where we spent the capital of our lives. We should prefer sound investment of our limited number of breaths to the goods of this world. We need to be like the travellers of virtue and truth, who give up the finite but embrace the infinite, preferring the right path to the path that leads to one's destruction.

O Allah! Provide us with pure and lawful sustenance and make us successful through our good deeds!

Amin!

10.

Light and Darkness

Allah the Almighty created man's perception and intelligence for him to understand reality by means of contrasts. We can comprehend the good by contrasting it with the bad, beauty through ugliness, right through wrong, and light through darkness. Hence human perception works by identifying objects and concepts on the basis of contrasts. We can only perceive the beauty and value of believing in Allah (*īmān*) through the ugliness of disbelief.

The Qur'an guides mankind towards the light of faith and away from the darkness of disbelief. Allah manifests Himself in two ways: one is His manifestation in the universe and the other His manifestation in the Qur'an. These two manifestations complement each other. The universe we live in is a Qur'an without words, and the Qur'an is a verbal universe. The universe is full of the divine secrets of Allah's greatness and the manifestations of His actions. Human beings are the essence of these two manifestations. Hence, Allah the Almighty clarifies this high position in the following hadith qudsī:

> O my servant! I have created you for Myself. And I have created all of the universe for you. My right over you is that what I have created for you should not engage you and make you heedless of Me. For you were created for Me (not for worldly concerns).

As a result of this, the Sufis refer to mankind as a microcosm and the essence of the universe. Man, because of his nature, inclines to both goodness and evil. There is both light and darkness in him. It is his responsibility to make sure that the light of faith is not covered by the darkness of disbelief. The Qur'an commands the believers to work for the victory of the light over darkness not only at the personal level but also at the social level, so that society can be saved from destruction. The Qur'an says: "Do they not travel through the land, so that their hearts (and minds) may learn wisdom and their ears may learn to hear? Truly it is not the eyes that are blind, but the hearts which are in the breasts." (*Hajj*, 22:46) The Qur'an further addresses heedless hearts: "Do they not then earnestly seek to understand the Qur'an, or are there locks upon their hearts?" (*Muhammad*, 47:24)

Those who can read and understand the pages of the Qur'an and the mysteries of the universe can see the manifestations of Allah in the external and internal world in proportion to the purity of their souls. Unfortunately, at times humanity behaves very heedlessly and darkens the divine realities out of ignorance and love of personal interests. Human beings idolize material benefits such as monetary wealth and worldly position. Hence, they leave the light of divine guidance and turn to the darkness of their *nafs*. In the Qur'an, Allah says that "Allah is the Light of the heavens and the earth." (*Nūr*, 24:35) Accordingly, those who reject Allah's way are left without light and they are blinded because of their rejection of the light of the Qur'an.

We can conclude that Allah wants us to lead a life in which we follow the divine light in all our everyday matters, whether social or personal, commercial or charitable, physical or spiritual. If we possess power over people as a ruler, or if we hold a position in government, we must always behave according to the divine

Light and Darkness

light that leads us to Allah. Human vices such as ignorance, laziness, tyranny and disbelief all lead to the darkening of the soul. Some of this darkness affects the personal life and some of it the social life. The Qur'an shows us the opposites of these traits, such as attaining knowledge, working hard, acting with justice and belief in the hereafter as the light of divine illumination. The prophets showed humanity the true nature of darkness as well as the correct code of behavior as a divine light which will ultimately lead us to the contentment of Allah.

Allah has never left humanity without a guiding light. The greatest lights that he bestowed on humanity is the light of the Qur'an and the light of our Prophet (upon him blessings and peace). History bears witness that the darkness of the *Jāhiliyyah* (the period of ignorance before Islam) was dispelled by the light of the Prophet (upon him blessings and peace). Hence, in order that we not return to the darkness of ignorance, we must follow the light of the Qur'an and the Messenger of Allah (upon him blessings and peace). Allah the Almighty says in the Qur'an: "Believe, therefore, in Allah and His Messenger, and in the light which We have sent down. And Allah is well acquainted with all that you do." (*Taghābun*, 64:8)

Those who do not lead a life in the light of the Qur'an are those who live in darkness. We must protect ourselves and our families from this darkness. The first step is to teach our children how to lead a life in accordance with principles of the Qur'an. In addition, we must teach them the pillars of Islam and the articles of faith. We must teach them all the good manners of Islam. The education process cannot be successfully completed within the family only, we also need to ask some professional help from qualified people. This might be local imams or Islamic schools and teachers.

The education process is very important in facilitating the perfection of human beings. It is like throwing healthy seeds into fertile lands; eventually they will produce the fruits of faith embedded in a Qur'anic lifestyle. In reference to this reality, the Prophet (upon him blessings and peace) states that we must encourage our children to perform daily prayer (*salāt*) after they are seven years old so that they get accustomed to worshipping Allah. This hadith indicates that religious education should start at an early age. The sincere advice and training given to the child is like engraving a piece of marble. If the love for Allah and His Prophet is cultivated in these little hearts, this beneficial influence continues throughout their lives.

One of the friends of Allah, Abū Bakr Warrāq sent his son to a school where they taught the Qur'an. One day his son came back from the school with a very pale face. Abū Bakr asked his son what the problem was. He replied, "O my father! Today in the school we learnt the following verse: "Then how shall you, if you deny (Allah), guard yourselves against a day that shall turn the hair of children gray?" (*Muzzammil*, 73:17) When I contemplated the meanings and warnings of this verse, I felt inside me great awe and I shook with fear."

After a short time his son passed away. Abū Bakr would often visit his graveyard and lament to himself, "For so long I have been reciting the words of Allah but, oh! How unfortunate I am that I could not comprehend the essence of this verse as my son did."

Truly the Qur'an is a mighty ocean that engulfs the childlike hearts of those who read it. Reading the Qur'an – the last revelation of Allah – is the best way of worshipping Allah. It is so important to recite the Qur'an in the *salāt* that if one does not read some parts of it in *salāt*, the prayer is not valid. Other essentials of the *salāt* such as standing or prostration can be left out in times of difficulty, but never the reading of the Qur'an. However, reciting the Qur'an should not be taken lightly for when a Muslim reads it. He or she should heed the following verse: "And recite the Qur'an in slow, measured rhythmic tones." (*Muzzammil*, 73:4)

The Qur'an also advises us to listen to the words of Allah in a careful manner: "When the Qur'an is read, listen to it with attention, and hold your peace so that you may receive mercy." (*A'rāf*, 7:204)

To be silent when the Qur'an is recited allows one to understand it, and understanding it leads to certainty of knowledge; this, in turn, invites divine mercy. The Prophet (upon him blessings and peace) also gave a good example in this respect. He would ask 'Abd Allāh b. Mas'ūd to recite the Qur'an and would listen to him with great respect and spiritual ecstasy from which his eyes would fill with tears.

Similarly it is a great bliss for parents that they listen to their children reading the Qur'an with a beautiful voice and pronunciation. Reading the words of Allah will lead them to become pious Muslims when they grow up.

Love and respect for one's parents is a strong natural inclination, but stronger than this is man's love for his own children. The strength of this emotion can overcome all other feelings. Hence, the Qur'an warns us not to neglect our parental duties towards our children. If parents educate their children according to Islamic principles, they become a blessing from Allah; otherwise they become a calamity (*fitnah*) for them. The Prophet (upon him blessings and peace) gives the following tidings for parents who have completed their duties towards their children by teaching them the Qur'an:

"The parents of those who read the Qur'an will be adorned with crowns of light and clad with garments of light (nūr)." (Abu Dawud, Ahmad, al-Hakim)

It is every married couple's desire at some time to have children; it is a strong drive in one's nature to do so. However, if one knew what bringing up children according to the principles of Islam entailed, they would think twice and would feel a daunting sense of responsibility. To raise children in an Islamic way is in effect to obey the Creator's divine will, since He created mankind in order that they worship Him. If one exerts oneself to the utmost of his ability, then even the worldly difficulties he suffers, such as working and being a breadwinner of the family – are counted as worship or forgiveness of one's sins. Children are shields between the parents and hellfire; they may save them from the fire. Our children are our most precious investment and the greatest blessing of Allah upon us. Hence we must protect them from all sorts of dangers, in particular the spiritual ones. Even animals protect their little ones from all sort of dangers with great acts of bravery. A mother hen, usually a very timid animal, behaves with extraordinary fierceness when its chicks are threatened.

But, you may ask, how are we to protect our children from harm and injury? Is it, for example, by feeding them with the best kinds of food, or should we satisfy their appetites with every kind of nutritious food? The true healthy diet our children need is that of spiritual food. It consists in firmly inculcating love for Allah and His Messenger (upon him blessings and peace) in their hearts. In this way they will carry out their religious obligations willingly and happily. Otherwise, they will perform their prayer irregularly and without any satisfaction. It is a pity that some Muslims do not teach their children their religion and the Qur'an, cutting themselves off from the light of the Qur'an. This is the greatest potential darkness looming in our children's future.

We must also be very careful when we choose spouses for our children. The first thing we must look in a would-be bride or bridegroom should be his or her Islamic upbringing and practice of Islam. Families based on non-Islamic foundations are destined to separate sooner or later.

In short, we must protect our children from the vices of our present society such as coming home late, wasting time and money, immoral films, and so on. Instead, we must fill their hearts with the love for Allah, His prophets and the upright friends of Allah. By this means alone can pure hearts make progress in the spiritual path by enjoying recitation of the words of the Qur'an and establishing the prayers voluntarily. They follow every detail of their religion with great care. Without love, prayers and worship are nothing.

Furthermore, the problems of society can only be solved by the moral system of Islam. Anarchy and crimes such as theft, rape and all other social diseases can easily be eradicated if we follow Islam. All these crimes are committed by those who cannot control their base desires, and Islamic morality is based on controlling one's actions and thoughts. The other big problem – selfishness and materialism – can also be treated by Islam, since Islam always commands sharing and thinking of the interests of others. Materialism can only grow when religion is absent; hence materialism is not a philosophy of life but rather a manifestation of the decline of mankind.

There are many non-believers in the society today who misuse their intelligence, or who do not know the limit of their five senses and where they must stop. Since they cannot understand religious facts they attempt to refute their existence. The Qur'an also answers the non-believers' mentality in their rejection of faith and the authority of Allah: "Does not man see that it is We Who created him from sperm? Yet behold! he stands forth as an open adversary!" (*Yāsīn*, 36:77)

These non-believers do not accept the reality of Islam because their hearts are dead. When a believer invites them to Islam, they say, "We are living in the age of science and reason, and what you are telling is the stories of the old times, nothing but superstitions." The Qur'an refers to such claims: "When their Messengers brought them clear verses they rejoiced in such knowledge as they had; but they were encompassed by that which they had mocked." (*Mu'min*, 40: 83)

The most important asset that we can pass on to our children is to educate them in such a way that they can wrest their next-worldly salvation from Satan's hands. We must send them to Islamic schools. Unfortunately, many Islamic schools around the world are on the brink of shutting down because of a lack of students. Most parents put money first when they choose schools for their children, and as a result very few of them decide to enroll Islamic schools. Nevertheless, only if our children gain a proper Islamic education can we solve the social diseases of our times such as anarchy, divorce, crimes rates and so on. Qur'an is the only cure for us as Allah says in the Qur'an: "We send down of the Qur'an that which is a healing and a mercy to those who believe. To the unjust it causes nothing but loss after loss." (*Isrā'*, 17:82) In another verse Allah says: "To Allah belong the treasures of the heavens and the earth; but the hypocrites understand not." (*Munāfiqūn*, 63:7)

Hence we should not give priority to worldly concerns, but rather our concern must be the place of our children in the hereafter. It is a weakness in the Muslim *ummah* that many do not follow the correct path in the education of their children because of their obsession with worldly interests. History bears witness that those who have followed the path of the Allah's messengers and the path of the prophets and people who are trustworthy (*sādiq*) and righteous (*sālih*), have achieved great worldly success as well as attained Allah's pleasure.

The Prophet (upon him blessings and peace) also informed us that Allah would elevate some nations because they followed the Qur'an, and destroy some others because of their rejection of the Qur'an. (*Muslim, Ibn Majah*)

The world can be compared to a large dining table laden with the most beautiful and exquisite kinds of food, which are the manifestation of two of Allah's attributes: the *Rahmān* and the *Rahīm* (the Beneficient and Merciful). We are sent into this world and we partake of and benefit from the delightful dishes of this banquet all due to grace of Allah. However, we must not ignore the fundamental truth that one day we will leave this banquet and will be questioned about our conduct around it. This means that we must abide by the rules of conduct and the etiquette laid down by the host – Allah. We should therefore follow the correct manners of eating and not plunder the food or overeat. Due to the mercy of Allah, everybody is given a place to eat at this table, whether it be a non-believer or a hypocrite or a good believer. However, one day, all of us will be held to account for our actions in the presence of Allah. We will be rewarded or punished according to our actions. We should take account of our actions before they are taken account of after we have passed on to the next world.

The Day of Judgement is not an ordinary day, but as the Qur'an describes it: "We only fear a day of frowning and distress from the side of our Lord." (*Insān*, 76:10) and "That day will man say: "Where is the refuge?" (*Qiyāmah*, 75:10). Allah, out of His boundless mercy for mankind, warns us of the perils and tragedies of that day so that we may not be caught unprepared:

> *O you who believe! Save yourselves and your families from a fire whose fuel is men and stones, over which are appointed angels stern and severe, who flinch not from executing the commands they receive from Allah, but do precisely what they are commanded. (Tahrīm, 66:6)*

The best of words is the word of Allah, and the best of the guidance is the guidance of the Prophet Muhammad (upon him blessings and peace). The best wealth that one inherits from his parents is knowledge of the Qur'an and the teaching of its commandments.

May Allah bestow upon us hearts which fear Allah and worship Him as though they see Him. May Allah also give us the power to follow the path of the Qur'an and the Prophet (upon him blessings and peace) which is the starting point of the trip whose destination is Paradise and the pleasure of Allah. May Allah also make it easy for us to attain the best morality of our Prophet Muhammad (upon him blessings and peace) in a spirit of Islamic brotherhood.

Amin!

11.

Excellence (*Ihsān*)[7] and Vigilance (*Murāqabah*)

Tasawwuf, or Islamic mysticism, means the full awareness of one's being in the presence of Allah at all times. Only those servants of Allah who have this sense of awareness can observe their duties towards both the Creator and His creatures. Every soul lives in the shadow of the reality that Allah is as near as stated in the Qur'an: "We are closer to him than his jugular vein." (*Qāf*, 50:16).

This state of awareness is called *ihsān*. One needs to be in a state of vigilance to protect this awareness. One who is in this position never forgets that they are being observed by Allah and that all their acts or thoughts are known to Him. To be in this position is like having a strong shield against sins; one cannot commit sins while his heart invokes "O my Lord!"

A person usually keeps away from sins in daily life if he knows that he is being watched by other persons, even if they are not able to punish him. Can such a person, who duly cherishes this feeling of *ihsān* and duly realises the vigilance of the Creator, act against the will of the Omnipotent? Not at all! Here is an excellent example in this regard from the time of the Companions of the Prophet:

---

7. *Ihsān* is defined by the prophet (upon him blessings and peace) as "It is to worship Allah as if you could see Him, for though you may not see Him, He certainly sees you." Hence this is a concept taken from the hadith of the Prophet (upon him blessings and peace).

The Secret in the Love for God

One night, Caliph 'Umar was wandering around the streets of Makkah as usual. He suddenly stopped when he heard a discussion between a girl and her mother. The mother was telling her daughter:

"O daughter! Dilute the milk we are going to sell tomorrow."

The girl replied to her mother:

"O mother! Has not the Caliph prohibited diluting milk?"

The mother shouted at her daughter:

"O daughter! How can the Caliph see that we dilute milk?"

But the girl, who feared Allah, did not agree to her mother's demand, and said:

"O Mother! Let us think for a moment that the Caliph does not see us. What about Allah? Do you think He does not see us? It is easy to hide this fraud from people but it is not possible to hide it from the Omnipresent Allah, Who is the Creator and the Sustainer of all being."

'Umar was moved by the words of this chaste girl, who feared Allah with a sincere heart. He was so deeply touched by her that he took her as a bride for his son, also a chaste person. 'Umar b. 'Abd al-'Azīz, who is considered the fifth rightly-guided caliph in Islamic history, was the son of these two chaste parents.

The main point here is that one should live in vigilance, being aware of Allah's presence everywhere. It is said in the Qur'an: "And He is with you wheresoever you may be. And Allah sees well all that you do." (*Hadīd*, 57:4).

Allah the Almighty is always with every creature at all times, He knows all the actions of His creation. He watches over them. To think that He is unaware of His creation presumes weakness in

Excellence (Ihsān) and Vigilance (Murāqabah)

Allah, Who is beyond any kind of weakness. If man knew this reality as he ought to, he could easily travel on the spiritual path. He would forget the concerns of this passing life and be interested only in the concerns of the spiritual life. The feeling of togetherness with Allah would keep man at all times in an awareness in which he can easily purify himself from worldly dross.

A friend of Allah says: "No traveller goes to sleep in the train station lest he miss the train. This world is like a train station to the next world. One needs to be awake to catch the right train."

To feel togetherness with God inspires one with awe from closeness to Him. It also comforts the believer to feel near Him. The following verse of the Holy Quran explains this closeness:

> *Do you not see that Allah knows whatever is in the heavens and whatever is in the earth? Nowhere is there a secret counsel between three persons but He is the fourth of them, nor (between) five but He is the sixth of them, nor less than that nor more but He is with them wheresoever they are; then He will inform them of what they did on the Day of Resurrection: surely Allah is cognizant of all things. (Mujadilah, 58:7)*

Again, 'Umar (may Allah be pleased with him) during his caliphate, sent Mu'ādh on a mission to the tribe of the Banū Kilāb. The purpose of the mission was to pay the necessary payments, deliver goods, and distribute alms which had been collected from the rich to be distributed among the poor.

Mu'ādh used to fulfill every mission with great care and come back with pleasant stories telling how he managed to win people's hearts. When he returned, he had only a piece of cloth to protect his neck from the sun and dust.

One day his wife asked him:

"Such people as you who undertake such missions are supposed to be paid and also get some presents for their households. Where are your presents for us?"

Muʿādh answered her: "There was an inspector accompanying me all the time in order to calculate what I take and what I give."

His wife became angry with him and said:

"The Prophet (upon him blessings and peace) trusted you, and so did Abū Bakr. Now, it is ʿUmar's time, and he sends an inspector with you. Does he not trust you?"

Her words were heard first by ʿUmar's wife, then by ʿUmar himself. ʿUmar called Muʿādh to ask him, reproachfully:

"What is this all about? Why do you say that I send an inspector with you? Do you not think I trust you?"

Muʿādh's answer was an exemplary one:

"O Commander of Faithful! This was only a story to tell my wife. In fact, the inspector that I was talking about was not you. It was Allah. Thus, I would not like to take something for myself in return for any service I did…"

ʿUmar understood what Muʿādh was saying, seeing that he was not interested in possessions. And he awarded him with a gift from his own possessions and said:

"Take this to your wife and appease her with this!"

The lesson to be taken from this story is that we should live in vigilance. We have to be aware all the time that our Lord is watching us. It is quite natural for one who works for charity

Excellence (Ihsān) and Vigilance (Murāqabah)

organisations to be paid for the work they do. Yet, the attitude of Mu'ādh is of great virtue. Those who work for charitable organizations may do extra work out of hours, as Mu'ādh did. Such people are therefore supposed to watch themselves from time to time to check their *nafs*; they should remember the following warning of 'Umar (Allah be pleased with him): "Take account of yourself before you have to account for yourself in the Divine Judgment."

The following saying of the Prophet (upon him blessings and peace) reminds us of the importance of remembering Allah and constant vigilance: "Do not waste your time with idle talk, forgetting Allah; because such talk that forgets Allah deadens one's heart. And it is such a person who is farthest from Allah." (*Tirmidhī*).

Therefore, we are supposed to be vigilant all day, whether it be before dawn (*sahar*), or when we awake for the early morning (*fajr*) prayer or during the daytime. The time must be a model for us to keep vigilance all day. Such a person who makes use of the pre-dawn time and daytime in order to win the happiness of his Lord is believed to be in the position of divine pleasure (*mardāt al-Rabb*). One who reaches this position eliminates all of the ill nature in their heart. It is as if the sunlight has been focussed through a lens to burn them; in the place of this ill nature, good nature arises through the divine attributes. This happens to such an extent that one is able to enjoy the expression of love, bounty, mercy, kindness, and forgiveness to all creation, with all due deference to the Creator. Such a person supervises their lower self in the best way. They observe the reason for their existence in this world with every breath, and take measures not to fall into the traps of Satan; their heart is always with their Lord. It is said in the Qur'an: "Know that Allah comes in between a man and his heart." (*Anfāl*, 8:24).

A servant of Allah who falls into this category enjoys the real taste of their trust in Allah. Their Lord has endowed them with direct knowledge; there is no middle man. Through this knowledge they begin to be able to read the pages of the universe. They grasp the wisdom and mysteries of existence. The Qur'an says: "So fear Allah – and it is Allah that teaches you." (*Baqarah*, 2:282).

It is this feeling of vigilance that saved the prophet Joseph from falling into the trap of a beautiful woman who tried to seduce him. He was saved from this trap through *ihsān* and vigilance. Therefore, the feeling of benevolence should be fixed in one's heart and should direct one's acts, enabling one to reach the position of being in union with one's Lord. Otherwise, merely uttering the words "benevolence" and "vigilance" will be of no use to the heart. The feeling of love has to be turned away from transitory beings to the Eternal Being. Once this feeling of love has been directed only towards Allah, the servant is able to take up the position of pious asceticism. When in this position, one undervalues worldly goods; their value comes through giving them away (*infāq*). The heart feeds its love of Allah with a pool of good deeds. Such acts give one's Lover (the Lord) pleasure.

A river that flows into the sea no longer keeps its own current or hue; it becomes, instead, under the control of the sea; it is no more a river. The same is true for *ihsān*: it is the person's annihilation in Allah, the manifestation of the Lord's attributes in the self.

Thus, we may say that benevolence is the core of faith. The results of this, such as sincerity, piety, and reverence in all prayers,

Excellence (Ihsān) and Vigilance (Murāqabah)

rituals, and invocations, can be gained only through benevolence. For every act of worship sends up shoots through the branches of sincerity, blossoms through piety, and finally bears fruit through reverence. To be on the right path means that one is aware of the Lord's omnipresence and acts accordingly, not only when in the company of people, but also when alone, feeling that the Lord is watching all the time. So, *tasawwuf*, with all its practices and forms, aims at empowering the heart to reach this position. Friends of Allah are students of this process throughout their lives.

One day Uways al-Qarānī was asked by his mother:

"O son! How can you manage to worship all night?"

Qarānī answered:

"O my dear mother! I worship Allah with great care. My heart broadens in piety so much that neither do I feel tired nor do I have any awareness of my bodily senses. I do not feel that the night is so long."

His mother asked:

"What is that thing called *khushū'* (pious reverence) in worship?"

He answered:

"It is to not feel the pain of the spear stabbed into one's body."

Again, here is another famous story from the history of Islam. During a battle, 'Alī was stabbed in the foot by a spear. The people around him tried to take it out, but they could not manage to do so because it was so painful. Then 'Alī said:

"Let me start praying and then you take it out!"

They did as he said and they were able to remove the spear easily. When he had finished his prayer, he asked them:

"What have you done?"

They answered:

"We have taken it out!"

As this case indicates, 'Alī's body felt nothing of this world; rather he was focussed on his spiritual joy because of the pious reverence during prayer. This is a clear and vivid example of benevolence and vigilance.

Taking pleasure in prayer and not being tired of praying can be possible only with a feeling of benevolence. One who has no feeling of benevolence in the heart feels tired when they pray. If such a person is rich, they will avoid giving alms because such a person cannot enjoy the pleasure of faith. Thus, we may conclude that prayers made in sincerity, alms given wholeheartedly, fasting performed joyfully, and pilgrimage performed lovingly are all outcomes of *ihsān*.

Being in the state of *ihsān* and vigilance is only possible through remembrance of Allah. It is this rememberance that makes the mind and heart connected with Allah, as well as fortifying one's wisdom. It is because of this reality that Allah said to Moses and Aarun when they were sent on a mission to the Pharaoh: "Go, you and your brother, with my signs, and slacken not, either of you, in keeping Me in remembrance." (*Ta-Ha*, 20: 42).

Many verses in the Qur'an enjoin remembrance of Allah. The following verse is enough to understand the importance of remembrance of Allah. Remembrance is the polish of the heart and it is the recipe for tranquility of mind, as the Qur'an states,

Excellence (Ihsān) and Vigilance (Murāqabah)

"Lo! Without doubt in the remembrance of Allah do hearts find peace." (*Ra'd*, 13: 28).

A heart that has been set at peace by remembrance of Allah is in the place where the divine attributes dwell. Such a heart is conscious of the secret expressed in the following verse: "The day whereon neither wealth nor sons will avail, but only he (will prosper) that brings to Allah a sound heart." (*Shu'arā'*, 26: 88-89). To attain such a position, one must overcome the barrier of the *nafs* and become mature through remembrance of Allah, and through repentance, pious resignation, patience, and vigilance.

We can summarize religion as consisting in two main aspects: legal aspects which are like the columns of a building, and pious reverence which is like the ornaments on these columns. *Tasawwuf*, which makes these two aspects come together, explains existence with wisdom. It opens up the spiritual windows to the miraculous event of *Mi'raj* (ascension to the heavens) of the Prophet (upon him blessings and peace).

Tasawwuf means to live Islam in observation of the values of sincerity, piety, reverence, submission, and love. In other words, it is taking a share from the life of the Prophet (upon him blessings and peace) as the Messenger of Allah, a time that lasted 23 years. As stated before, *tasawwuf* means acting in accordance with the Allah's commandment to the believers, made through the person of the Prophet (upon him blessings and peace) in the verse "Therefore stand firm (in the straight path) as you were commanded." (*Hūd* 11: 112). As mentioned before, this verse made the hairs of the Prophet turn white.

It is worth noting that the Prophet, during the 23-year period after the Qur'an was first revealed, participated in many battles and went hungry for many days. He lost Khadhīja, his wife, and

Hamza, his uncle who had protected him from the idol worshippers, and five of his six children died in his own lifetime. He accepted all this suffering in humble submission. However, the Prophet (upon him blessings and peace) said that it was the chapter of the Qur'an, Hūd, which contains the verse "Continue then in the right way as you are commanded…" (Tirmidhī) that had aged him.

The path of reaching Allah is a long and narrow one with many difficult tests and distractions lying in wait, such as one's passions. This path contains great responsibilities, which are so great that they even turned the hair of the Prophet white. The friends of Allah refer to their incapability of being perfect servants of Allah in the face of endless divine manifestations, as follows: "O Lord! We have been unable to know You as You deserve…"

In the light of this fact we should, in the matters of *ihsān* and vigilance, be aware of our Lord's constant observance over us before directing our lives to the way of our Prophet who lived as the symbol of benevolence and vigilance. How patient was he, and how patient are we? How generous and loyal was he, and how generous and loyal are we? How devout was he in prayer, fasting, almsgiving, and the declaration of faith, and how devout are we? How committed was he in the service of the right path, and how committed are we? These are the questions that we should answer sincerely. In short, we should organize our life in the light of all these comparisons to the ways of the Prophet (upon him blessings and peace) who is the best model of righteousness for humanity until the Day of Judgment and thus our foremost witness and intercessor in both worlds.

In order to reach states of *ihsān* and *murāqaba* we should prepare our hearts by purifying our *nafs*, allowing it to submit to us with ease. We should be among those who are mentioned in the following verse: "Truly he succeeds that purifies it." (*Shams*, 91:9)

The following are among the things that should be carefully observed:

- To be careful about legitimate earnings.

- To observe the rights of human beings and other creatures of Allah.

- To spend the pre-dawn hours (*sahar*) worshipping Allah.

- To do what is enjoined by Allah and refrain from what is forbidden.

- To take on responsibilities in social service.

- To give alms for the sake of Allah.

- To be in the company of sincere and pious people.

- To be touched by the words of the Qur'an and to serve the Qur'an.

- To practice invocations from the bottom of our hearts.

- To avoid immoral acts such as backbiting, egoism, selfishness, extravagance, lying, jealousy, ambition, hypocrisy, and other such acts.

- To remember death and breathe in awareness of Allah until our last breath.

Without doubt the Prophet Muhammad (upon him blessings and peace) is the best model for us in setting an example of how one should live a life of *ihsān* and *murāqaba*. After him come the heirs of the Prophet – the friends of Allah – and they are to be followed in this regard as well. Mahmud Samî Ramazanoğlu, whom we lost just over twenty years ago, is one of the most memorable examples in this regard. He lived a life adorned with *ihsān* and *murāqaba,* and he enlightened his disciples in this way. We commemorate him and pray for Allah's mercy and grace on him.

May Allah help us to conduct our lives in a benevolent and vigilant way.

Amin!

12.

Mankind's Reality

Allah the Almighty has provided everything in the world for the service of mankind (*Jāthiya*, 45:13); however, He has also declared that mankind bears certain responsibilities (*Qiyāma*, 75:36). He has adjusted the general flow of life by setting a fine balance between freedom and responsibility by means of divine rules for the universe, as well as for those of mankind. In the following verse of the Qur'an, Allah the Almighty orders humanity to unite in harmony with the universe: "And the firmament has He raised high, and He has set up the balance (of justice), in order that you may not transgress the due balance." (*Rahmān*, 55:7-8)

Yet, those who are unaware of the secret of our existence in this world, cannot be in harmony with the divine order and beauty Allah the Almighty has created, because they are too attached to worldly pleasures and temporal things. Unfortunately, such people waste their lives, falling into heedlessness and ignorance.

This secret is hidden in the reality of human beings, who are equipped with two opposing tendencies, good and evil. These tendencies were given to human beings as a divine test which can only be possible with the existence of alternative choices and different characters that may tend to good or evil. In order for human beings to make their good tendencies the dominant traits in their lives, their mystical and intellectual faculties will not be sufficient. If they were, Allah the Almighty would not have made Adam the first prophet of mankind, and would not have bestowed the divine truths upon him, which guided him to comfort and peace in this world and the hereafter.

Indeed, all of the mystical and intellectual faculties of mankind can easily be manipulated towards either good or evil. One of those faculties, for instance, is the rational mind. It is like a double-edged sword that can commit deeds which are either sinful or virtuous. The best stature (*ahsanu taqwīm*) cannot be attained without using reason only. Nevertheless, this same mind can bring human beings lower than even the status of beasts. It is therefore necessary for the human being to bring discipline to the use of reason. This can be achieved through the guidance of divine revelation; in other words, by following the teachings of the prophets. If a person allows divine revelation to guide the mind, that person can attain true peace. If not, they will be led astray. Therefore, the mind needs to be guided by the direction of Allah's will.

Throughout history, many arrogant people used their reasons very effectively for the purpose of harming others. They justified their actions by assuming that these bad deeds were the most logical and reasonable thing to do. For instance, when Hulagu Khan invaded Baghdad and drowned 400,000 people in the Tigris, he was not troubled by his conscience. Before the coming of Islam, the people of Makkah used to bury their daughters alive, silencing their heart-rending screams. They were not troubled by what they did, and they did not stop carrying out that terrible act. Rather, it was to them like felling a tree; they would argue that to do so was their legitimate right.

Mankind's Reality

All of these people had minds and feelings. Nevertheless, like a wheel that spins counter-clockwise, they had gone in the wrong direction. These examples show that human beings are creatures who need direction and guidance; they possess both positive and negative traits. If this guidance is not given under the direction of the prophets, the faculties of human beings lead them astray, turning them into murderers and deluding them into thinking that they had done the right thing. A mind without guidance is like a dark cloud veiling the conscience and blocking feelings of compassion and mercy.

Allah the Almighty has sent prophets in order to reveal the proper way, and to show us how urgently mankind needs advice, guidance and great personalities to uplift them. Indeed, the blessing of Islam and the guidance of the Prophet Muhammad transformed the cruel people of the *Jāhiliyya* (pre-Islamic age of ignorance) who buried their daughters alive, into merciful people, who would weep if they witnessed the slightest injustice.

Allah the Almighty has created some human beings with distinguished qualities, such as the Caliphs. As previously stated, He bestowed upon people both the soul and the ego, both of which are in a continuous struggle. This is the test. Thus, the most virtuous creation, human beings, find a place between the lower stage, occupied by animals, and the upper stage, occupied by angels. They find their exact place according to their efforts and their struggle between their soul and their *nafs*. Thus, of all creatures, man stands the most in need of purification (*tazkiyah*), and attaining good morals *(tarbiyah)*. Allah the Almighty says in the Qur'an that a life far away from *tazkiyah* and *tarbiyah* is like that of an animal, perhaps even lower: "Many are the Jinns and men we have made for hell. They have hearts wherewith they understand not, eyes wherewith they see not, and ears wherewith they hear not. They are like cattle, nay more misguided: for they are heedless (of warning)." *A'rāf*, 7:179)

The dual weakness and wealth of man stems from the severe contradictions found within his inner and outer life. Man has accepted the trust *(amānah)* that the mountains refused to accept, because they feared the responsibility. These are contradictions that are difficult to overcome. This is because a human being possesses virtues that elevate him to be near Allah, and at the same time deadly vices that keep him far from Him. People with no *tarbiyah* or peace in their hearts store up animal characteristics in their inner world. Some are sly like foxes, some are rapacious like hyenas, some are as hard-working as ants, some, too, are as poisonous as snakes. Some nibble lovingly, some suck blood like leeches, some smile while stabbing their friends in the back. All of these are different characteristics of animals. Every human being who cannot be free from his or her *nafs* and cannot eventually establish a good character, is overwhelmed by his or her own evil traits. Some people may have only one animal characteristic, while others may have more. It is not difficult for knowledgeable people to recognise them; faces reflect what lies inside.

People with positive traits and people with negative traits live side by side in this world. An analogy of this situation is that of a gazelle kept in a stable of vicious and wild animals, with whom it must live. Sometimes, a miser lives side by side with a generous person, an imbecile next to a wise man and a compassionate person with a stone-hearted man. Misers are merciless, they are cowards and shy away from giving service to others. Imbeciles cannot understand the wise; cruel people assume that they are being fair but always abuse their power. Those with angel-like souls live next to evil people. The former try to recognise the truth (*haqq*) and be good servants while the latter live according to their instincts, and think that happiness is to eat, mate and attain a high social status.

To live in a world full of opposite personalities is a difficult test for human beings. Yet we are required to pass this test, and this is in fact our true aim in this world. In order to pass this test, it is necessary to develop good morals rather than bad traits. We must bring virtuousness into our being.

The human body comes from earth and there will it return. As we possess some of the qualities possessed by other creatures, it is a must that we control ourselves using *tazkiyah* and *tasfiyah*; otherwise, there will be no escape from the evil of *nafs* within us, which weakens the soul. In the Qur'an, Allah states: "By the soul, and the proportion and order given to it; and its inspiration as to its wrong and right; truly he succeeds that purifies it, and truly he fails that corrupts it!" (*Shams*, 91:7-10)

Rūmī explains the concepts of right and wrong in the following exhortation: "O traveller of truth! Do you want to know the truth? Neither Moses nor the Pharoah are dead. They are alive in you. They are hidden in you. They keep fighting each other in you! So look for them in yourself!"

Again Rūmī says:

Do not feed your body to excess, because it is a sacrifice that will be given to the earth in the end. Instead, try to feed your soul. It is the one that will go to the heavens and be honored.

Give your body small amounts of tasty food, because those who give it too much become the slaves of their nafs, and eventually have an unpleasant future.

Give your soul spiritual food; give it mature thinking, fine understanding and spiritual food, so that it can go where it is supposed to go in as capable a way as possible.

The *nafs* with no spiritual training (*tarbiyah*) resembles a tree with rotten roots. The signs of decay can be seen in the branches, the leaves and the fruits. Likewise, if a heart has a disease, it is reflected in the body as bad traits, like hatred, jealousy and arrogance. These bad traits are tied to the *nafs*. In order to cure this disease one must abide by Allah's commands.

However, for those who are at different levels in life and have different characters there is a need for guidance by model personalities; the most essential foundations in establishing the character are imitation and emulation.

13.

Selflessness (*īthār*)

During a journey, 'Abd Allāh b. Ja'far (may Allah be pleased with him) stopped by a date orchard. The caretaker of the orchard was a black slave. Somebody had just brought three slices of bread to the slave, when a dog came by him. The slave gave one slice of the bread to the dog. The dog ate it. Then, the slave gave him the second slice. The dog ate that too. He gave the last slice of bread to the dog and the dog ate it. 'Abd Allāh, having witnessed what had happened, asked the slave, "What is your wage?"

The slave replied:

"My wage is the three slices of bread, as you saw."

'Abd Allāh then asked:

"Why did you give it all to the dog?"

The slave replied:

"Usually there are no dogs around here. This dog must have come here from afar. I could not let him go hungry."

'Abd Allāh asked:

"But what are you going to eat today?"

The slave replied:

"I will be patient. I have turned over my day's earnings to this hungry creature of Allah."

'Abd Allāh said:

"*Subhān Allah*! People say I am very generous. This slave is more generous than I am!"

Following this, he bought the orchard and the slave. He gave the slave his freedom and donated the orchard to him. (The story is narrated in *Kimyā-i Sa'ādah* by Imam al-Ghazālī)

Islam, out of which such kind, compassionate and tender people have emerged, has made *zakāh* (poor tax) obligatory to forestall enmity and jealousy, and to maintain social equity and love between the poor and the rich. It also encourages voluntary charity, which is a conscientious obligation to establish Islamic brotherhood at a higher level. Thus, Islam allows each believer to develop a rich heart while enabling him to reach the zenith of selflessness. After confirming the oneness of Allah, the real goal of the religion is to establish peace in the society by raising kind, considerate and thoughtful people. This perfection is attained only through the feelings of affection and compassion which reside in the heart, and as their consequence give rise to the ability to share one's earnings regardless of one's own needs. Rising beyond this, these feelings may nourish the desire to share all that one has. This is what we call *īthār* (selflesness) in Arabic.

Mercy is a fire that is never extinguished in the heart of a Muslim. In this world, it is the distinguishing essence of being human which leads us through the heart to union with our Lord. A compassionate Muslim is generous, humble, and a person of service. At the same time, he is a doctor of hearts who injects life into the souls of others. A compassionate believer is a person who strives at all times to offer all of his or her services with love and compassion, and is a source of hope and faith for the people around him or her. A believer is always on the first line of every struggle which bestows peace to the hearts of others. Likewise,

Selflessness (īthār)

with their words, acts, and presence, believers undertake a constructive role against every type of misery, suffering and pain. They are always at the side of the sorrowful, troubled, abandoned and hopeless, because the first fruit of faith in a Muslim is mercy and compassion. Human morality and values are perfected with the Qur'an. For this reason, when we open the Qur'an, the first divine attributes that we come across are the Most Merciful and the Most Compassionate. Our Lord gives us the good tidings that He is the most compassionate of the compassionate ones, and He orders His servants to embody the qualities of His morality. In turn, a believer's heart which is filled with love for their Lord must project mercy and compassion towards all of Allah's creatures. The consequence of loving Allah is to turn towards His creatures with love and compassion. A lover of Allah conceives of making sacrifices as a pleasure, and as a measure of the degree of his love for the Beloved.

Thus, giving charity for Allah's creation is an expression of love for Allah. Indeed, there are many kinds of *sadaqa* (charity for the sake of Allah). The highest point of giving, as we mentioned above, is *īthār* (selflessness). This is the quality of putting the needs of others above one's own needs. Selflessness is the highest level of sensitivity which every mature believer is obliged to conscientiously reflect upon in his social conduct. Entering the flourishing climate of selflessness is only possible with a kind heart and a kind soul, because real selflessness is giving without fearing poverty. This state is exhibited to perfection and in a most beautiful way in the lives of prophets and the friends of Allah. Of course, it is not for everyone to climb to such a zenith and reach such high stars. But, based on the reality that the closer we can get to these horizons the more blessings we earn, even the smallest step in the path of selflessness is an eternal gain that cannot be abandoned.

According to the narration of Abū Hurayra (may Allah be pleased with him), a man came to the Prophet (upon him blessings and peace) and said: "O Prophet of Allah! I am hungry!" The Prophet (upon him blessings and peace) sent somebody to one of his wives and they asked for some food. But the mother of the believers said, "I swear by Allah Who sent you as a Prophet that there is nothing at home other than water." Upon hearing the same thing from his other wives, the Prophet (upon him blessings and peace) turned to his Companions and asked: "Who wants to have this person as a guest tonight?" Someone from the Ansār, said, "I will have him as my guest, O Prophet of Allah!" and he took that poor man to his home. When they arrived at the house he asked his wife: "Is there anything to eat?" She said: "No, there is only enough food for our children." The companion said: "Then keep the children busy. If they want food, put them to bed and make them sleep. When the guest arrives, turn off the light. We will pretend to be eating." When the guest arrived they all sat down for food. The guest ate and satisfied his hunger, whereas they only feigned to eat. Since there was no light the guest did not see that his hosts were not eating. They slept in hunger. In the morning the companion went to the Prophet (upon him blessings and peace). When the Prophet saw him, he said, "Because of what you did for your guest last night, Allah is very pleased with you." (*Bukhārī, Muslim*).

Even though Sheikh Mahmud Sami Ramazanoğlu, a friend of Allah, had a degree in law, he did not practice this career out of fear of violating a person's rights. Instead, he preferred to be a bookkeeper at a store in Tahtakale, Istanbul. He would cross the Bosphorus to Karakoy by boat, and from Karakoy to Tahtakale he

Selflessness (īthār)

used to walk instead of taking the bus. By making this sacrifice, he was able to give his bus fare as charity. The states of consciousness and morals of the great personalities are beautiful examples for us. Even by making small sacrifices in personal comfort, in the decoration of our homes, or in our daily expenses, we can adopt their example and share in their high morality.

Selflessness (*īthār*) at the same time extends beyond generosity (*sakhāwa*), because generosity is sacrificing wealth that is not needed. Selflessness, however, is giving something that is needed. The spiritual rewards of selflessness are in proportion to the sacrifice of the servant. Allah praised the Ansār who turned over their wealth to the Muhājirūn (those Muslims who fled persecution in Makkah) and chose to take care of their needs before their own needs as is said in the following verse: "But they give them preference over themselves, even though poverty was their own lot. And those who are saved from the covetousness of their own souls, they are the ones that achieve prosperity." (*Hashr*, 59:9).

Once when 'Umar b. Khattāb (may Allah be pleased with him) was on his way to Jerusalem, and it was his servant's turn to ride the camel, he insisted that his servant stay on the camel even though they had arrived at the entrance of the city. They entered Jerusalem with the servant riding the camel and 'Umar was walking. This is an example of *īthār*, or selflessness. This shows that charity is not always monetary. The actions described above are also kinds of charity.

Selflessness, which is the highest level of charity, is in essence tearing something off from oneself and giving it out, turning over one's share to his brother in religion. It is a special kind of charity that belongs to Prophets, Companions, friends of Allah, and righteous servants (*sālihūn*).

The following incident involving ʿAlī b. Abī Tālib (may Allah be pleased with him) and his noble wife Fātima (may Allah be pleased with her) demonstrates selflessness in the best way: Ibn ʿAbbās (may Allah be pleased with him) narrated that ʿAlī and Fātima fasted for three days to fulfill their pledge to Allah when their sons Hasan and Husayn recovered after an illness. The first day they cooked a dish with barley flour for breaking their fast, and just as they were about to break their fast there was a knock at the door. It was a poor person who was hungry. The family gave the food they had to this person willingly for the sake of Allah and they broke their fast with water only. The second day, when it was time to break their fast an orphan came to their door. They gave their food to this orphan and broke their fast with water again. The third day, a slave came to them asking for help. They showed great patience and selflessness and gave their food to the slave.

This unparalleled generosity, selflessness and beautiful morality was confirmed and extolled by the following verses, where Allah said:

> *And they feed, for the love of Allah, the indigent, the orphan, and the captive, (saying), "We feed you for the sake of Allah alone: No reward do we desire from you, nor thanks. We only fear a day of frowning and distress from the side of our Lord". But Allah will deliver them from the evil of that day, and will shed over them brightness and a (blissful) joy. (Insān, 76:8-11)*

Selflessness (īthār)

None among Allah's creations can be compared with the Prophet (upon him blessings and peace) regarding generosity, charity and selflessness. His generosity was far beyond the generosity of ordinary people. He was generous with his knowledge, his wealth and his soul, through sacrifice in the path of Allah, explaining the religion, leading people to the right path, feeding the hungry, advising the ignorant and helping the needy while relieving their burden. (*Altinoluk Sohbetleri*, V.III, p. 56).

Safwān b. Umayya, who was one of the most well-known pagans among Quraysh, was with the Prophet (upon him blessings and peace) during the wars of Hunayn and Tā'if, even though he was not a Muslim. While they were walking in Jirāna, the Prophet (upon him blessings and peace) saw that Safwān was looking in surprise at some of the booty that had been collected. He asked Safwān: "Do you like it?"

When he answered "Yes" the Prophet (upon him blessings and peace) said: "Take it! It is all yours." Upon this, Safwān took *shahāda* and became a Muslim, saying, "No heart other than the heart of a Prophet can be this generous." (*Islam Tarihi*, p. 474).

Selflessness is the most magnificent level of generosity. We have to remember that through such generous actions of the Prophet, his Companions, and the righteous servants of later generations (May Allah be pleased with them), many people who were stubborn in their denial became believers; many enemies became friends. Likewise, selflessness strengthened the love of many believers for their fellow believers. The Prophet of Allah (upon him blessings and peace) never refused a request if it was in his power to fulfill it. Once he had ninety thousand dirhams. He put them on a mat and distributed them to every needy person who came by.

The Quality of Giving Freely (*birr*)

The quality of being able to give freely, which is called *birr* in the Qur'an, is also a noble charity like *īthār*. The Prophet (upon him blessings and peace) who is the ideal example of all moral qualities, is a matchless great personality in this way too. The following story shows his sensitivity to giving preference to his Muslim brother over himself even in the smallest thing. One day the Prophet (upon him blessings and peace) made two toothbrushes from a *miswāq* (a stick for brushing the teeth). One of them was very nice and straight, the other was crooked. The Prophet (upon him blessings and peace) gave the better one to his companion and kept the crooked one for himself. When his friend said, "This nice one is better for you, O the Messenger of Allah!", the Prophet (upon him blessings and peace) said: "The person will be questioned who accompanied someone even for an hour whether or not he was careful about the rights of friendship." This way he showed that this right is only paid with the understanding of *īthār* and *birr* by choosing the need of a Muslim brother over his own (*Ihyā' 'Ulūm al-Dīn*, V.II, p. 435).

The following story is another example of this kind of charity. One day the Companions were gathered around the Prophet (upon him blessings and peace) in the mosque and they were listening to his sermon. The Prophet (upon him blessings and peace) recited this verse: "By no means shall you attain righteousness unless you give (freely) of that which you love: and whatever you give, Allah knows it well." (*Āl 'Imrān*, 3:92)

The Companions who were listening to the Prophet (upon him blessings and peace) felt this verse in the depths of their hearts. They were trying to reckon if they were capable of giving what they liked the most. Suddenly a companion stood up. This

Selflessness (īthār)

companion, whose face was bright with the light of faith was Abū Talha (may Allah be pleased with him). He owned a big garden with six hundred date trees in it that was very close to the Prophet's Masjid and he loved that garden very much. He used to invite the Prophet (upon him blessings and peace) to his garden often and get his blessing.

Abū Talha said: " Messenger of Allah! Of my property, that which I love most is the garden in the city which you are familiar with. At this moment, I wish to give it to the Messenger of Allah for the sake of Allah. You can dispose of it the way you see fit and give it to the poor." After he spoke he went to the garden to carry out this decision. When Abū Talha reached the garden he found his wife sitting under the shade of a tree. Abū Talha did not enter the garden. His wife asked: "O Abū Talha! Why are you waiting outside? Come in!" Abū Talha said: "I cannot enter inside, you should also take your belongings and leave." Upon this unexpected answer his wife asked in surprise: "Why, O Abū Talha, is not this garden ours?" "No, from now on this garden belongs to the poor people of Medina," he said and gave the news of good tidings in the verse and told her eagerly of the act of charity he had performed. His wife asked, "Did you give it on behalf of the two of us or just yourself?" He answered, "On behalf of us." He heard the following words from his wife in peace: "May Allah be pleased with you, Abū Talha! I thought of the same thing when I saw the poor people around us, but I could not find the courage to tell you. May Allah accept our charity. I am leaving the garden and coming with you, too!"

It is not difficult to predict the kind of climate of happiness that would surround the world if this moral quality became rooted in the souls of people. Imagine the beauty that would come out of this. This is what led Abū Talha to make such a sacrifice.

The Messenger of Allah (upon him blessings and peace) encouraged even those who had very little to give charity. For example, even though Abū Dharr (may Allah be pleased with him) was one of the poorest Companions, he used to encourage him to give charity by saying, "O, Abū Dharr! When you cook soup, put in plenty of water and share it with your neighbors!" (*Muslim*, Birr, 142).

A believer must give out light like a full moon on a dark night, and be considerate, sensitive, kind, selfless, generous, merciful, compassionate, and full of enthusiasm for giving charity. There is a serious need for giving charity and being selfless in these days of economic crisis. We should not forget that we could be the ones struggling in poverty and need. For this reason, it is our debt of thanks to Allah to give charity to the ill, sorrowful, lonely, needy and hungry people and act in a selfless manner. We should share the bounties we have with the needy, so that those hearts which we fill with happiness will be a means of our spiritual progress in this world and a source of reward and happiness in the hereafter and happiness. O my Lord! Let all kinds of mercy be the endless treasure of our spiritual life.

Our Lord! Guide us to be embodiments of the selfless life of our Prophet Muhammad (upon him blessings and peace) and living manifestations of the selfless lives of the scholars of Islam who have followed his example!

Amin!

14.

Islam Gives Life to Mankind

The Prophet Muhammad (upon him blessings and peace) embraced a society that was engulfed in violence and injustice. Through his personal conduct, which radiated endless mercy and love, he transformed a society full of hatred and revenge into a loving and caring social system. Before his arrival, people were brought up to abuse the young and the weak, and to attack others for the pettiest reasons. However, after seeing the conduct of the Prophet (upon him blessings and peace) the people who had perpetrated these acts purified themselves and abandoned their cruel attitudes. These same people became the embodiment of mercy and love and developed the capacity to guide the rest of humanity by virtue of their example. Like stars that illuminate the world on dark nights, they reflected the beauty of Islam. The following story of Mus'ab b. 'Umayr is one of many such examples:

One day Mus'ab and his friend As'ad b. Zurāra went to the tribes of 'Abd Ashhal and Zafar in order to invite them to Islam. The chieftains of these clans were Sa'd b. Mu'ādh and Usayd b. Hudayr. Sa'd asked Usayd: "Why do you not prevent these individuals from coming here and cheating the poor and simple among our people"?

Upon this Usayd met Mus'ab and Zurāra, and pointing his spear at them roared, "If you wish to stay alive, leave this place immediately!"

Instead of reacting angrily, Mus'ab replied, "If you calm down and listen to me, I have a message for you. You are a man of high intelligence and wisdom. If you like what I have to tell you, you may accept; and if you do not, you may reject all that I have to say."

Usayd agreed and put his spear away. After listening to Mus'ab's beautiful words about Islam, he himself accepted Islam. Then he went back to his friend Sa'd and said, "I have listened to what they have had to say and have found nothing wrong with their words."

Sa'd was unhappy with his friend's approval of the unwanted guests, and thereafter personally went to Mus'ab, his sword half sheathed, and ordered them to leave. In the same manner as before, Mus'ab did not reply with harsh words and instead brought peace to the situation with nice words, and spoke about the realities of Islam with deep wisdom. Like his friend Usayd, Sa'd also accepted Islam under the influence of the divine attraction of the message he had just received.

This is an example of how the Arab people lost their aggressive character in the process of accepting Islam, and how they were transformed through the conduct of the Prophet Muhammad (upon him blessings and peace). The Arabs ultimately cultivated the highest states of patience and maturity. They understood that Islam had come to revive people and not to destroy them, and they engraved the following words in the pages of history: "Those who come to kill are in need of spiritual revival."

Rūmī also notes that they knew that in the face of mercy and goodness, evil is powerless:

When the seas of mercy begin to surge, even stones drink the water of life,

The frail mote becomes stout and strong; the carpet of earth becomes satin and a cloth of gold,

He that has been dead a hundred years comes forth from the grave; the accursed devil becomes an object of envy to the houris on account of his beauty,

The whole face of this earth becomes verdant; the dry wood blooms and flourishes,

The wolf becomes the cup-companion of the lamb; the despairing become courageous and valiant". (Mathnawī, V, 2282-85)

The Prophet Muhammad (upon him blessings and peace) forgave many criminals who would have been executed. He even forgave Wahshī, who killed his beloved uncle Hamzah (may Allah be pleased with him). The Prophet's (upon him blessings and peace) mercy and love for human beings always exceeded his anger. Many a wrathful person melted in the abundant love of the Prophet and they were transformed into rose-gardens of mercy. A Turkish poet described the situation in Arab society before the time of the Prophet (upon him blessings and peace) thus: "If a human being had had no teeth, his own brothers would have gobbled him up." By this is meant that people were merciless even towards those closest to them. Islam has saved humanity from such deep ignorance and brutality.

The cruel people of that society became so merciful that the following situation emerged in the battle of Yarmuk in which some of them were wounded. When the wounded were offered water before their last breath, each gave up his turn to the other and refused to be the one to drink the water first. As the opportunity to drink was passed from one to the other, all of them passed away before any one was actually able to quench his thirst.

The Prophet (upon him blessings and peace) always led the caravan of love and mercy from the very front, and ceaselessly displayed moral conduct at its peak. As a result, friend and foe alike acknowledged his exemplary character. In the last century in The Hague, Holland, scholars and thinkers gathered to select the hundred most important people who had contributed to the betterment of humanity. They chose Prophet Muhammad (upon him blessings and peace) as the first and foremost person according to the principles they had chosen in making their selection. Interestingly enough, the selection committee consisted solely of Christians. It is also interesting to note that ninety percent of the Companions of the Prophet (upon him blessings and peace) accepted Islam because they had appreciated his high moral qualities. Even those who were extreme in their enmity towards him were unable to accuse him of being a liar or a despot, but rather were forced to praise him.

Those who have given their hearts to Islam and would like to serve the religion should know that Islam aims first and foremost at reviving humanity. Only those who can perceive the beauty of Allah's creation in each human being, and who realize that Allah has created human beings as the most valuable objects of His creation can serve Islam and humanity in the way Allah wishes. In other words, the ideal of Islam is to facilitate the emergence of ideal human beings. This ideal may only be realized when the heart of the perceiver has been touched and reawakened, and the spiritual beauties hidden within it have begun to resurface.

Islam Gives Life to Mankind

As a result, Islam has always emphasised as its first priority the spiritual education of Muslims, and many great personalities have appeared in the history of the *Ummah* who were admired by all people regardless of their beliefs. Through the Prophet's (upon him blessings and peace) example and teaching, those who had been under the control of their *nafs* and led a bestial life became angelic stars, dazzling eyes with their brightness. For example, 'Umar b. Khaṭṭāb, who had before Islam buried his daughter alive, later became a source of mercy incapable of harming even an ant. Islam thus represents a spirit that embraces humanity with love and mercy. Through the seeds of this endless mercy it has sown into the hearts of man, human beings were raised up to exceed their limited and weak natures. They became able to reach towards eternal life.

Islam came to revive people. The emotions and feelings Islam teaches are the essence of humanity. The famous Turkish Sufi poet Yūnus Emre said:

Let us befriend one another

Let us make things easy

Let us love and earn the love of others

No one will remain in the world forever

Those who have not integrated their allotted share of divine love and mercy into their souls are the enemies of both humanity and their own souls. These merciless people have blocked their path to spiritual nourishment and fulfilment. On the other hand, the great friends of Allah who have arrived at the spring of mercy – such as Jalāl al-Dīn Rūmī and Yūnus Emre – are loved by all as the roses of Paradise. Even in the worst of conditions they have the capacity to spread hope and cure the wounds of society. The nature of the rose is the most important characteristic that all Muslims should have: it gives off its sweet scent among sharp thorns. Instead of embracing the characteristics of the thorn, the good believer should be like the roses that bloom after the long winter months. Rūmī said in reference to this: "He that sows the seed of thistles in the world, be warned not to look for him in the rose-garden" (*Mathnawī*, II, 153). Rūmī continues:

> *You are observing defects on the face of the moon – picking thorns in a Paradise!*
>
> *Picker of thorns, if you go into Paradise, you will find there no thorn but yourself. (Mathnawi, II, 3347-48)*

Our ancestors, the Ottomans, were very merciful to their captives after battle. A captive officer once said: "O mercy, you are such a tyrant that you make me love my enemy!"

It is unfortunate that nowadays some materialists and rejecters of faith have confused Islam with terrorism. This is one of the most terrible calamities that humanity has ever experienced. Terrorism is the result of a lack of love and mercy as the hearts of terrorists never lodge such sublime feelings. Islam is a religion of the heart and terrorists have nothing in this center since their hearts were hardened like rocks. Islam from its inception rejects all sorts of terrorism and anarchy. It commands the respect of the rights of both Muslims and non-Muslims without discrimination.

The Prophet (upon him blessings and peace) used to send teachers to the tribes who wanted to learn about Islam. Once in an incident called Bi'r Ma'ūna the unbelievers trapped these teachers on their way to the tribe and killed them. After this, the Prophet (upon him blessings and peace) always sent some soldiers to protect the teachers. He commanded these soldiers only to use their weapons for the protection of the teachers. However, once Khālid b. Walīd, who was the commander of such a battalion, used his weapon out of necessity and harmed some people and their possessions. Having heard of this incident, the Prophet (upon him blessings and peace) said, "O my Allah I am innocent of what Khālid has done. I am not happy with what he has done." He repeated these words three times. After this, he sent 'Alī to pay compensation for everything, including the dogs of the tribe who had been harmed. (*Islam Tarihi*, I, 525-27)

The Ottomans too adopted the high morality of the Prophet (upon him blessings and peace) in their stance towards non-Muslims, and they never forced non-Muslims to accept Islam. They never attempted to destroy other nations, or to change people's cultures through imperialistic acts. Rather, they considered non-Muslims to be fellow human beings whose rights they were to protect. Because of such tolerance, the people in today' Poland said: "We will never obtain freedom unless the Ottoman horses drink water from the Vistul river..."

Thus, the oppressed people of other nations preferred Ottoman rule to that of their own rulers. When the Ottomans besieged Constantinapole, some Byzantine noblemen suggested that they should ask for help from the Pope. It is interesting to note that one of the nobleman, a man named Notaras, said, "I would rather see Ottoman turbans than the miters of cardinals in Constantinople."

Today in the Islamic world we need to adopt this traditional Islamic mentality in which we love people just for the sake of their Creator. This is not for political reasons, but rather to gain the pleasure of Allah.

The following story is a good example of the mercy Sufis showed to Allah's creation. Once, during one of his travels, Abū Yazīd al-Bistāmī paused under a tree and ate some food. Then he continued on his way. After some time he saw an ant on his food bag. He realized that the ant had climbed on the bag when he paused under the tree. He felt very sad to think that he had removed the ant from his home. He went all the way back and returned the ant to its original home. He was aware that the rights of Allah's creation, even an ant's, needed to be respected even as much as those of a human. Islam engenders such a great heart in Muslims that even an ant is treated with the utmost mercy. Such a person will naturally protect the rights of his fellow human beings more than anything else. But such a way of life will only be possible if man develops his spiritual capacities, making him the envy of angels rather than feeding his *nafs* through which he may fall to a state even lower than that of beasts.

The world today is confronted by a great deal of injustice and the killing of innocent people. This is the consequence of a process in which human beings have followed their base desires and ignored their spiritual development. In the end this has resulted in the loss of those sublime feelings such as love and mercy for others. The solution for those who have thus lost themselves is to discover the truth and depth of Islam and surrender themselves to its call while understanding that the beauty and glamor of this world will not last forever.

This world is only a preparation for our everlasting life in the hereafter. The famous Turkish Sufi and lover of Allah, Yūnus Emre said in one of his famous poems: "Love the creation of Allah for the sake of its Creator." Is not this all-encompassing verse the best cure for tyrants who are in need of mending their ways before entering the bliss of the hereafter? If those people were able to cultivate a small share of Yūnus Emre's love for humanity, they would never be able to perpetrate the horrible crimes they have committed. If they were only able to heed this verse, they would instead be blessed with feelings of love and justice towards humanity rather than the enmity of the dark side of their *nafs*.

We must proclaim that Islam should not be abused for the political aims of some people. Hence, we should carefully separate the religious and pious people from those who use religion to attain their own evil ends. In Islamic history we have witnessed groups like the Khawārij, who killed innocent people in the name of Islam because their sole aim was to attain political power. We have also witnessed in the past some states who have used Islam to justify their evil aims. Evil people, in order to realize their unjust plans, use the valuable feelings and concepts of religion only to advance their personal desires and as a consequence defame both religion and religious people. However, as Rūmī has said, they will pay a high price for their evil acts:

> *Most people are like predators; put no trust in such people when they say "Peace to you."*
>
> *Their hearts are the house of the devil; do not listen to the chatter of devilish men.*
>
> *He that swallows "lā hawla" from the breath of the devil, like the ass falls headlong in the fight. (Mathnawī, II, 251-53)*

Rūmī continues to warn the pure hearts of innocent people from the dangers of such evil-doers:

He utters vain words to you who says, "O my beloved", that he may strip the skin off his beloved like a butcher.

He gives vain words that he may strip off your skin; woe to him that tastes opium from enemies. (Mathnawī, II, 258-9)

Heartless terrorists use their humanity only as a mask to veil their merciless hearts which have never tasted divine love. If such people were ideologues, they would promulgate ideas that would only pollute people. If they were poets, they would poison the souls of others. If they were moralists, they would propagate immorality. Rūmī has revealed the real nature of this type of people in the following words:

If he takes a rose in his hand, it becomes a thistle;

and if he goes to a friend, he bites him like a snake. (Mathnawī, II, 154)

In short, such people are killers of souls. They take joy in blinding people's eyes and paralysing their sensibility. By employing all sorts of inhuman methods such as drugs, they transform human beings into merciless beasts. Instead of cultivating genuine human logic and reason, they provoke only people's feelings of revenge and their aggressive side. They have consistently been the worst enemies of humanity throughout history. Allah the Almighty describes the attitude of such people as follows: "When it is said to them: 'Make not mischief on the earth.' They say: 'We are only the ones that put things right.' Of a surety, they are the ones who make mischief, but they realise (it) not." (*Baqara*, 2:11-12)

Islam Gives Life to Mankind

No one can claim that butchering civilians is a religious act and no one can confuse it with *jihād*. As a matter of fact, only those who use religion to justify their evil plans are the ones who have lost the pleasure of Allah. Allah the Almighty has explained the grave consequences of their actions in the following verse:

> On that account We ordained for the children of Israel that if any one slew a person—unless it be for murder or for spreading mischief in the land—it would be as if he slew all people. And if any one saved a life, it would be as if he saved the life of all people. Then, although there came to them Our messengers with clear signs, yet, even after that, many of them continued to commit excesses in the land. (Mā'idah, 5:32)

The Holy Qur'an considers the killing of one innocent person to be equivalent to killing all of mankind, for such a killer in fact attacks the sacredness of human life itself. If one kills an innocent person this implies that he might kill all of humanity for his own personal pleasure. In such an act, he sets an example for others to do the same and thus encourages murder. Hence, killing innocent people is one of the biggest crimes in Islam, and those who commit such acts attract the wrath of Allah in the hereafter. On the other hand, if someone saves a life, prevents a crime or removes the causes that may lead to manslaughter, such a brave person is considered in principle to have saved all of humanity.

Rūmī likens Islam to the water of life and states that no one dies near the water of life: "None ever died in the presence of the water of life." (*Mathnawī*, VI, 4218)

All the rules and principles of Islam aim at conserving and protecting human life in both physical and spiritual terms. In all instances, Islam guides humanity to correct belief and good conduct, and it cultivates in people feelings of mercy, love of service to humanity, love of wisdom, courtesy, kindness and respect for justice.

In particular during the holy month of Ramadan, Islam supports Muslims with a very special spiritual atmosphere. During this month Muslims are privileged to fast, to pray *tarāwīh* (extra night prayers), and give charity generously to the poor. Through fasting, the arteries which are blocked by the diseases of mercilessness are opened and cleaned, and hearts are inclined to the weak, needy and lonely people.

Ramadan is a month of mercy. In cultivating mercy, a Muslim can practice Islam with greater depth since he reins in his base desires as he strives to bring them under control. In this process, the soul is refined and becomes more sensitive to divine openings. The fruits of mercy are forgiveness, generosity, and modesty. As we serve others, we learn gradually to give up jealousy. All these difficult achievements are made easier during the holy month of Ramadan. Our souls exceed their limitations as we struggle to serve the divine command to extend our care to all humanity, and in this universal spirit of service the soul strives to reach the perfection of its Lord.

In short, achieving true felicity in Islam is dependent upon both faith in the oneness of Allah and undertaking meritorious acts. Good Muslims dedicate their hearts and minds to Allah as they dedicate their lives to the service of humanity and thereby learn to cultivate virtuous lives. Rūmī describes this attitude as follows:

Oh, happy is the ugly one to whom the beautiful one has become a companion, alas for one of rosy countenance with whom autumn consorts. (Mathnawī, II, 1341)

O my Lord! Make this and the next world a place of felicity through the beauties of Islam. Protect the Muslim *ummah* from all kinds of mischief and disaster.

Amin!

15.

The Significance of Manners in *Tasawwuf*

One of the Companions of the Prophet, Abū Dardā', was appointed as a judge in Damascus. Because of his post, he had come across many criminals. One day he pronounced his judgment concerning a criminal and the case was concluded. However, he heard those who were present cursing the guilty man. Upon hearing this Abū Dardā' asked those who were cursing:

"What would you do if you saw a man who fell into a deep well?"

They answered, "We would send down a rope to save him."

"In that case why don't you strive to save this man who fell into a pit of sin?"

They were surprised by this statement and asked, "Don't you hate this sinner?"

Abū Dardā' gave this wise response, "I am not the enemy of his personality but of his sin."

Abū Dardā' wanted to provide a lesson for the believers. Abū Dardā's wisdom is a reflection of the Prophet's (upon him blessings and peace) morals, and these reflections are the most perfect principles gathered together in the essence of *tasawwuf*. This wisdom does not let the sinner drown in his sins. Rather, it gives the sinner a chance to repent and to be purified in the sea of mercy, love and forgiveness. The Prophet (upon him blessings and peace) behaved in this way even with Abū Jahl, who was among the idol-worshippers who were harshest in their enmity. Instead of punishing him by exposing his sins, he always invited him with kindness to salvation and purification in the divine sea of mercy.

Allah the Almighty shows His deep love and mercy to those who repent. If a sinner repents, Allah forgives all his or her sins and cleanses his or her past. Allah even turns those sins into good deeds, depending on the sincerity of the person. Allah the Almighty says concerning those who repent: "Unless he repents, believes, and works righteous deeds, for Allah will change the evil of such persons into good, and Allah is oft-forgiving, most merciful." (*Furqān*, 25:70)

Those who have not taken their share of divine love and mercy are the enemies of both themselves and humanity. These people have blocked their path toward spiritual nourishment. In stark contrast are the great friends of Allah who have attained the spring of mercy, people such as Jalāl al-Dīn Rūmī and Yūnus Emre. They are the roses of Paradise who are loved by all righteous people. Even in the worst conditions they give hope and cure the wounds of society. As already mentioned, this is an important characteristic which all Muslims should have. Abdullah Rūmī Eşrefoğlu explains the Sufi path thus: "For the friend's sake, one should be able to swallow poison like sugar."

Mahmud Sami (May Allah have mercy upon him) also gave us a good example of mercy and love towards sinful Muslims. One day one of his students, due to depression, came to his house and knocked on his door. He was completely drunk and in no condition to come to the door of a sheikh. The one who opened the door was angry at this attitude and frowned at him. He asked,

"What are you doing? Aren't you aware of whom you are visiting?" The poor man answered, "Is there any other place, which will welcome me like this house will?" The Master Mahmud Sami overheard this conversation and came to the door. He let the student inside the spiritual palace, consoled him, and helped him solve his problems. He cured his wounded heart with mercy and love. This kind treatment helped the man to overcome his difficulties and he repented from his sins. He later became a spiritual and pious man.

The Sufi approach to human beings is positive and friendly. Rather than peering into their sins and highlighting their negative characteristics, Sufis examine the good essence of the person, and strive to develop these innate aspects. However, this approach should not mislead us; it does not mean that Sufis are permissive of people being sinful. Sufis do not tolerate the existence of sin. But they approach sinners with mercy and love, and in that way they strive to win over their hearts in order to help them. For Sufis, a sinner is a person like a bird with a broken wing; such a person attracts their mercy and compassion. Their aim is to help the sinner and to console his or her wounded soul. They do this purely for the sake of Allah, and it should be remembered that showing love and care for the sake of Allah is one of the most effective ways of attaining spiritual perfection. The following is narrated by 'Umar b. al-Khattāb (may Allah be pleased with him):

During the lifetime of the Prophet (upon him blessings and peace) there was a man named 'Abd Allāh whose nickname was *Himār* (Donkey), and he used to make the Prophet laugh. However, on several occasions the Prophet had him lashed for drinking alcohol. One day he was brought to the Prophet (upon him blessings and peace) on this charge and was lashed. At that, one man among the people exclaimed, "O Allah, curse him! How frequently has he been brought [to the Prophet] on such a charge!" The Prophet (upon him blessings and peace) said, "Do not curse him, for by Allah, I know that he loves Allah and His Apostle." (*Bukhārī*)

Human beings have a high position in all creation just because they are human. Bad actions and characteristics do not change this exclusive position, because every man and woman carries the divine *nafkha* (breath, essence) from Allah. The divine essence always stays with man although most sinners are not aware of their value and their place within the divine order. To give an example, it would be as though the Black Stone fell into the mud. There is not a single Muslim who would not lament such a situation and run to restore the Black Stone to its sacred place. They would clean it with their tears and polish it with their beards. Muslims show due respect and love even if the black stone is covered in dust and dirt. They remember its origin and high value since it came from Paradise. It is also the same for human beings. They came out of paradise (i.e. our father Adam) and whatever sin they commit, this divine essence never departs.

Similarly, a good doctor never gets angry at the flaws of his patient. The diseases occur due to a person's ignorance, laziness, and other shortcomings. However, a good doctor looks at the pain and suffering of their patient and does not look at their shortcomings. The doctor immediately runs for the patient's treatment and does not waste time getting angry with the patient. In the same way, the Sufi is like a spiritual doctor and, when the Sufi sees a spiritual disease among the members of society, they hurry to cure it rather than complain. The Sufi is like a life-jacket in a spiritual storm. It is a duty and causes happiness to give a drowning man a life-jacket even if that man actually fell into his predicament through his own fault. The Prophet (upon him blessings and peace) said after the battle of Khaybar: "O 'Alī! It is better for you [as far as the divine recompense is concerned] to guide one man to Islam than to have everything over which the sun rises and sets."

Allah the Almighty showed the significance of saving one person from destruction in the verse we already mentioned above: "And if any one saved a life. It would be as if he saved the life of all people." (Mā'idah, 5:32)

The worst sin a person can commit is to associate partners with Allah and the rejection of Allah's existence. The cure for this grave sin lies in a soft and tolerant approach. When Allah the Almighty sent Moses (upon him blessings and peace) to Pharoah, He commanded him to speak softly and kindly (*qawl layyin*) with Pharoah. Guiding someone to Islam successfully is the greatest achievement for a believer and a bridge to their salvation. Allah the Almighty was not unaware of the level of infidelity of Pharoah when He commanded Moses to deal with him softly. Why? Because Allah wanted to teach us the manner in which we should preach Islam.

We must always be kind and gentle when we tell others of Islam, even if our opponent is like Pharoah in his enmity towards Islam. We should not be ruled by our emotions or be rough with the non-Muslims. Threatening, cursing, and other such kinds of behavior are not the Islamic way of preaching Islam. Highlighting this reality, Rūmī says in his *Mathnawī*: "Understand well the words of Allah to Moses: 'Speak nicely to Pharoah and treat him in a friendly manner!' Because, if you add water to boiling oil you only increase the fire, and destroy both the pan and the oil."

The Significance of Manners in Tasawwuf

The following verse of the Qur'an addresses us, the *Ummah* (community of Muslims), with regard to the personality of the Prophet, upon him blessings and peace:

It is part of the mercy of Allah that you dealt gently with them. If you were severe or harsh-hearted, they would have broken away from about you: so pass over (their faults), and ask for (Allah's) forgivenesss for them; and consult them in affairs (of moment). Then, when you have taken a decision, put your trust in Allah. For Allah loves those who put their trust (in Him). (Āl 'Imrān, 3:159)

Among many other verses which teach us the way of telling others about Islam and calling to it (*da'wa*), the following verse occupies an important place: "Invite (all) to the way of your Lord with wisdom and beautiful preaching; and argue with them in ways that are best and most gracious: for your Lord knows best who has strayed from His path and who receives guidance." (*Nahl*, 16:125)

This tolerance and gentleness should be shown not only to the sinners, the rejecters of the faith, but also to the good believers. We are all human beings, and even those who practice Islam in the best possible way sometimes make mistakes. If we use a harsh method when we correct someone else's mistakes, this can even be counter-productive. Instead of curing the other person, we could cause him or her to be even worse due to our impolite and coarse treatment. Human nature detests rude treatment. Even sons and daughters do not accept their parents' rough treatment, and a very useful piece of advice loses its value if it is given in a disrespectful way.

We should not forget the fragile psychology of the human being, and never treat a sinner rudely – regardless of the number of sins they have committed. Our treatment should remind them of the self-value they possess, and help them to recouperate their divinely-given spiritual powers. The Prophet (upon him blessings and peace) strongly warns us that being disrespectful towards a believer is a sin, and we should never disrespect someone due to his or her bad state. He said: "It is a grave sin for a believer to disrespect his Muslim brother." (*Abu Dawud, Musnad Ahmad*)

Bezmiālem, an Ottoman noblewoman, in order to protect the personality and integrity of servants, established a foundation in Damascus to compensate them for any damage they might have caused in their work places. By doing so, the servants and working people would not feel very bad when they broke something.

In preaching Islam, we must always show gentleness and mercy towards others and redirect criticism and responsibility to ourselves. Allah the Almighty says: "And enough is He to be acquainted with the faults of His servants." (*Furqān, 25:58*) In another verse Allah says:

> O you who believe! Avoid suspicion as much (as possible): for suspicion in some cases is a sin. And spy not on each other, nor speak ill of each other behind their backs. Would any of you like to eat the flesh of his dead brother? Nay, you would abhor it... But fear Allah: For Allah is oft-returning, most merciful. (*Hujurāt, 49:12*)

Those who bring into practice these verses are the epitomy of morality and virtue. Such people have well understood that this world is not separate from the other, since we all travel from here to there. Osman Gazi – the founder of the Ottoman state – was one of those who lived in conformity with these verses. His master Sheikh Edebali one day gave him the following advice:

O my son! You are a king now. From now on getting angry with you is our share and your part is to be tolerant. When we are cross with you, it is your duty to gain our hearts back; when we blame you, it is your part that you must be patient. When we are wrong and weak, it is your part to be helpful and tolerant of our mistakes. When we are in trouble and in disagreement with each other, it is your duty to be just with us. When we talk unjustly and criticise you, it is your duty to forgive us... O my son! From now on when we fall into disunity, it is your duty to unite us. If we become lazy, it is your duty to work and urge us to work hard.

This is priceless advice for rulers – when they are treated badly they must forgive others for the sake of Allah. They must always show mercy and love towards their subjects under all circumstances.

When the Prophet (upon him blessings and peace) wanted to point out a certain mistake that a person had committed, he would talk about the mistake, but would not reveal identity of the person who had committed it. While he would teach the community about the mistake, he would not offend anybody in doing so. He would ask: "What is happening to me that I see you committing this or that [mistake]?", as if he had attributed to himself the fault of seeing things wrongly.

This is a common practice among Sufis, so as not to offend the person who had committed the sin. This is because the path of Allah is a path to win hearts and build them up, not break them. The famous Sufi poet Yūnus Emre states this fact in the following verses:

The heart is Allah's throne:

Allah looks into the heart.

The unfortunate of the two worlds

Is the one who broke a heart!

Forgiving guilty Muslims and responding with kindness to those who harm and offend are the most important characteristics of a good believer. A good believer even prays for the well-being of believers who are criminals, praying for their souls in both this world and the hereafter through repentance. The Prophet (upon him blessings and peace) showed the greatest example of this mercy and compassion. When the people of Tā'if stoned him, instead of asking their punishment, he asked for their forgiveness. He never prayed to Allah for the destruction of the people who had harmed him. He also prayed for the forgiveness of the people of Makkah, who had showed him the greatest enmity to the Prophet (upon him blessings and peace). Through his prayers, many tyrants became good Muslims. The Qur'an informs us: "Nor can goodness and evil be alike. Repel (evil) with what is best, when lo! he between whom and you was enmity would be as if he were a warm friend!" (*Fussilat, 41:34*)

The Prophet (upon him blessings and peace) also explains that it is not a good thing to do good only in return for good, or to do evil in return for evil, but rather when you do goodness in return for a wicked act committed against you. (*Tirmidhī*)

When we behave as described in the hadith, our enemy becomes our friend. If the person is our friend, his or her friendship increases and he or she comes even closer. Today in the western world people are turning to mystical movements in order to escape from the merciless attacks of materialist philosophies, because the materialist lifestyle is destroying the humanity of mankind. It is therefore beneficial and more merciful to employ the principles of *tasawwuf* when inviting western people to Islam. Many western people who have become Muslims have read the works of Rūmī and Ibn 'Arabī to satisfy their spiritual needs. It is also a fact that in the western world today among the most popular books are those which deal with *tasawwuf*. Hence we should heed the call of Rūmī: "Come! Come! Whoever you are come, even if you are a non-believer, a fire worshipper, a pagan! Our lodge is not the house of hopelessness, come even if you have broken your repentance a hundred times."

We need the all-embracing mercy and love spelled out by Rūmī. His call to tolerance aims at introducing human beings to their divine nature and bringing them to Islam through the mercy and compassion of Allah. Rūmī does not mean by these words to accept all the kinds of mistakes people make and let them stay in the same state without any correction. His aim is to cure the people's spiritual world. The hearts of the great Sufis are like repair shops where broken hearts are repaired. Thus, his call is directed not towards perfect Muslims but to the errant and heedless ones. Especially in times when the religious life is weak and people are ignorant, we need the great Sufis' approach in our invitation to Islam – selfless love, mercy and tolerance. This is the only viable way of saving those who are surrounded by all kinds of spiritual afflictions, and have drowned in the sea of disobedience to Allah.

On the other hand, it must be strongly pointed out that tolerance of sinful people can be applied in personal encounters. Sinners cannot be tolerated if their sins are harmful to society and destroy its order. Those who commit tyranny and destroy the fabric of society for their own personal interests do not deserve our love and tolerance. It is also not a bad thing that ordinary people detest sin and the sinners. They want to escape from sin wrought through this kind of extreme behavior, and this is necessary for them in order to refrain from sin. For heedless people, sin is like siren music which lures and makes it very easy to commit. Hence, to regard sin lightly has two harmful effects. The first is that one can easily fall into sin, and the second is that belittling the sin causes Allah's wrath. In other words, we must tolerate the sinner, not the sin itself. The following hadith narrated by Anas b. Mālik explains this: The Prophet said, "Facilitate things for people [concerning religious matters], do not make it hard for them, and give them good tidings and do not cause them to run away [from Islam]." (*Bukhārī*) Of course this should be done without harming the essence of the religion and without straying from the straight path.

O our Lord! Please place us among those who have attained wisdom and divine love. Make our hearts a source of love and mercy towards the creation of Allah for the sake of Allah. Replace our sins and ugliness with beauty and divine reward. Make our people live in peace and mutual love and protect us from all sorts of calamities and disbelief.

Amin!

16.
Love (*mahabbah*)

Love is the joy, pleasure, tranquility and taste of our fleeting life. Love is the yeast in the dough of existence. For one to be able to love is among our Lord's greatest gifts to His servants. Love should, therefore, always be oriented towards worthy objects. It should be used for those hearts that truly understand friendship. This phase in love for human beings and the creatures of this world is a step towards attaining divine love. Yet, unfortunately, most human beings sacrifice love, which is a divine gift, for their momentary and egotistical desires.

The love that does not encounter the one who truly deserves it is sadly the greatest loss in this life. Love that is in the grip of cheap worldly interests is like a beautiful flower growing between the cracks of the pavement; sooner or later it is destined to be trampled underfoot and die. How unfortunate for a diamond to be dropped and lost on the street! And what a deep and sad loss for it to be the property of an undeserving person!

The great Sufi master Jalāl al-Dīn Rūmī sets forth the following instructive example as an illustration of those who are deprived of divine love as a result of sacrificing their wealth of love for transient and worthless things:

> *Those who love this world and dedicate their hearts to it resemble a hunter who is trying to catch a shadow. How can a shadow belong to him? Similarly, a foolish hunter confuses the shadow of a bird with the actual bird itself*

and tries to capture it. Even the bird on the branch of the tree is amazed by what the shadow-hunter is trying to do!

The hearts in which the seeds of love do not grow cannot be saved from their destruction. Enslaved by egotistical feelings, in a way they carry the corpse of spiritual feelings. Yet, the love that is nourished from the divine spring of the spiritual abode is like the flowers of Paradise which exude a beautiful fragrance. Even if sometimes their flowers turn pale and the leaves fall down, all it takes is a smile from the spring to revive and rejuvenate them again.

Those who attain divine love, which is the very source of love, can befriend other living beings. In other words, they gain the ability to look at these living things with the vision of the Creator. The friends of Allah who reach this zenith cleanse themselves from all kinds of egotistical pleasures and live with an understanding that true pleasure is in knowledge and love of Allah. It is stated in a hadith qudsī:

> ... My servant draws not near to Me with anything more loved by Me than the religious duties I have enjoined upon him, and My servant continues to draw near to Me with supererogatory works until I love him. Then, when I love him, I become his hearing with which he hears, his seeing with which he sees, his hand with which he strikes, and his foot with which he walks..." (Bukhārī).

This spiritual zenith is as rare as the peaks of the tallest mountains on earth. Those who make this divine grace and blessing the definitive element of their personality are saved from becoming an ordinary person. Such people have a unique way of speaking with the living creatures in the world. The only

Love (mahabbah)

requirement by which this can be achieved is the acquaintance of the heart with the language of those creatures!

For those who can hear, there are many different songs that emanate from a singing nightingale, a delicate flower, or a cascading creek. The night air can tell countless stories. For those who are aware, how many different breezes do the morning winds carry? The perfect believers, whose hearts are full of love and compassion, are those who can observe with a deep understanding the flow of divine secrets and wisdom in this world. Would it be possible for a healthy mind and a living heart not to be touched by the burning songs of divine love after having witnessed all these divine secrets and magnificent works of art?

The value of love is commensurate with the importance and perfection of the beloved. Accordingly, the summit of human love is love for the Prophet Muhammad (upon him blessings and peace), for it is impossible to imagine another human being who deserves to be loved more than he does.

Yet, even the Prophet Muhammad (upon him blessings and peace) is not the last station for love. For a human being, the ultimate destination for their love should be Allah, the Creator of all being. The last phase and final destination in the ascension of a human being through spiritual love is Allah. The Sufis call this station, *fanā' fi Allāh* and *baqā' bi-Allāh*. This state is similar to rivers that reach the ocean and merge and disappear into it.

A great friend of Allah reflects in his poetry the burning with the fire of *fanā' fi al-Rasūl*[8] and *fanā' fi Allāh* as follows:

---
8. *Fanā' fi al-Rasūl* means emptying the heart of those qualities that contradict the Sunnah of the Prophet Muhammad (upon him blessings and peace) by subduing the ego.

O my Beloved! From the manifestation of your beauty, the spring is enflamed!

The rose is on fire, the nightingale is on fire, the hyacinth is on fire, the soil and the thorn are on fire!

Your light, which is bright like the sun, is what burns all lovers!

The heart is on fire, the chest is on fire, and those crying two eyes are on fire!

Is it possible to wash the corpse of the martyr of love with all this fire?

The body is on fire, the coffin is on fire, and the cool sweet water is on fire!

Attaining the love of Allah requires the achievement of true love for the Messenger of Allah; this is the final stage of human love prior to divine love. For this reason, those who do not experience love for the Messenger of Allah (upon him blessings and peace) will not be able to experience love for Allah. One should know that the only stream of love and mercy that leads to the ocean of divine love is the love for the Messenger of Allah (upon him blessings and peace). Love for the Messenger of Allah (upon him blessings and peace) is love for Allah; obedience to him is obedience to Allah; and disobedience to him is considered rebellion against Allah. Consequently, the blessed existence of the Prophet Muhammad (upon him blessings and peace) is the sanctuary of love for all humanity. As is stated in the Qur'an: "Say: 'If you do love Allah, follow me: Allah will love you and forgive you your sins. For Allah is oft-forgiving, most merciful.'" (Āl 'Imrān, 3:31).

Love (mahabbah)

There is no doubt that the greatest sign of love is submission and sacrifice for the sake of the Beloved. The extent to which a lover conforms with the beloved depends on the degree of love in his heart. If there is love in the heart, there is also sincerity, purity of intention and divine blessing. The deeds of a human being attain a higher value if they are performed out of love. In contrast, the deeds that are not performed out of love are pretentious, lack sincerity and only strengthen egotism.

Even a small deed performed out of love is incomparably superior to outwardly monumental but insincere deeds. The most important manifestation of this can be observed in divine love that is the peak of all loves. The highest and the most perfect level for a servant is to attain the blessing of divine love. Yet, there is no doubt that love, like everything else, is also created by Allah the Exalted. Therefore, without His permission, a servant can never reach this level. Therefore, the responsibility incumbent upon a servant is to pray, supplicate, and seek refuge in Allah. The Qur'an states: "Say (to the rejecters): 'My Lord would not concern Himself with you but for your call on Him. But you have indeed rejected (Him), and soon will come the inevitable (punishment)!'" (*Furqān*, 25:77).

The sign of love for Allah and the path to reach His love is to perform supererogatory deeds out of divine love and compassion with great respect, kindness and joy even though one is not required to do so, after performing one's obligatory duties with deep reverence. Continuing in this state until one attains divine love means the realization of the purpose of the creation of humanity, as the ultimate goal of all religious duties is to reach the presence of Allah. The most important means for this is love for Allah. All other deeds are merely manifestations of this love.

The Secret in the Love for God

It is normal that when the love for Allah increases in the heart of a believer, the amount of his good deeds for the sake of Allah also increases. That is why those who make progress in love for Allah do not feel content by simply performing obligatory deeds; instead, they want to increase their deeds by performing voluntary deeds with the same care and joy by which they perform obligatory deeds. As a result, their desire for good deeds increases in the same way that the desire for water increases in the desert. Nothing can comfort people in this state except returning to Allah. As is stated in the Qur'an: "(To the righteous soul will be said:) O soul in complete rest and satisfaction! Come back you to your Lord, well pleased and well-pleasing unto Him!" (*Fajr*, 89:27-30).

The believers who have reached this level of divine love certainly strive to turn their entire life and every breath into worship; they pray to Allah in secluded places and in the darkness of the night, far from people's praise. With a ceaseless awareness of being a servant of Allah, they try to quench their thirst with the drink of love in the abode of *ihsān* which, as we said, means to worship Allah as if one can see Him, and to live with the awareness that Allah is watching one's actions at all times. On this way they may, if required, sacrifice their wealth, status, all worldly belongings, and even their life. Above all, they continuously make supplications in their heart requesting Allah's love and pleasure.

The following incident from the life of 'Ammār b. Yāsir (may Allah be pleased with him) illustrates well the love of the honorable Companions of the Prophet Muhammad (upon him blessings and peace) for Allah and their complete submission to His will:

Love (mahabbah)

While walking on the shore of the Euphrates, prior to a battle, 'Ammār expressed his inner feelings as follows:

O my Lord! If I knew that You would be happier with me if I were to throw myself from the top of that mountain, I would do it right away. If I knew that burning myself in a large fire would please You more, I would do it immediately. O my Lord! If I knew that throwing myself in the water and drowning myself in it would please You more, I would do it instantly. O my Lord! I am fighting with the sole purpose of seeking Your pleasure. I ask You not to let me lose. I wish to attain Your pleasure!" (Tabaqāt Ibn Sa'd).

Love for Allah and His Messenger (upon him blessings and peace) is the essence of our religion and the most blessed path to Allah; it is the only means for divine mercy and friendship. Achieving love for Allah is the highest level in reaching the presence of Allah, because the gate to the divine presence is only opened by the key of love. However, love should not be mere rhetoric. Empty talk, which does not reflect what is held within the heart, has nothing to do with true love for Allah. Worse, it brings about only self-aggrandisement.

The most concrete examples of true love were demonstrated by the great Companions. They became the living examples of the love for Allah and His Messenger in their daily lives and missions. Some of the examples are as follows:

The Messenger of Allah (upon him blessings and peace) sent teachers to the tribes who resided in the vicinity of Medina. The tribes of Adal and Kare were among the tribes who requested teachers. A group of ten teachers set off for the tribes. On the way they were ambushed. Eight of the teachers were martyred in the conflict and the remaining two were captured. The tribes who captured these two Companions, Zayd ibn al-Dathina and Khubayb ibn 'Adi (May Allah be pleased with them) turned them over to the polytheists of Makkah who put them to death. Prior to killing them, the polytheists asked Zayd, "Would you trade places with Muhammad so that you could save your own life?" Zayd looked pityingly at Abū Sufyān who asked the question and said, "Not only I do not accept to be with my family and children, but I cannot even consent that his foot get hurt by a thorn!" (Abu Nu'aym, *Ma'rifat al-Sahaba*)

Abū Sufyān was stunned by this matchless proof of love. He said, "I am indeed surprised! I have never seen in this world people who love someone more than Muhammad's companions love him."

After this, the polytheists went to Khubayb and told him that if he were to abandon his faith he would be saved. The response of the great Companion Khubayb was clear, "I would never leave my religion even if you were to give the entire world!" Khubayb had only one wish before being martyred: to send his greetings with love to the Prophet Muhammad!

Yet, who could take this greeting to the Prophet? Powerless, he turned his eyes to the sky and prayed with utmost sincerity: "O my Lord! There is no one here to convey my greetings to Your Messenger. Convey my greetings to him!"

At that moment, the Messenger of Allah, who was in Medinah with his Companions, uttered the words "'*Alayhi al-salām*," which means "May the peace and blessings of Allah be unto him." Hearing this, the Companions were surprised, and

Love (mahabbah)

asked, "O Messenger of Allah! whose greetings were you answering? He replied, "The greetings of your brother Khubayb!"

The polytheists of Makkah killed both Companions after cruelly torturing them. The last words of the great Companion Khubayb were very significant, "As I am martyred as a Muslim, I do not care in what way I receive my death" (*Bukhārī*).

Likewise, because of their love for the Messenger of Allah (upon him blessings and peace) the young Companions competed with each other for the honor of serving as his envoy, carrying his missionary letters. With the intention of fulfilling even one of his wish, they requested services that they could offer him, even if it required a great sacrifice on their part. It is a clear indication of their infinite love for the Messenger that, after crossing endless deserts and high mountains, they read out the letter of the Prophet in the presence of kings with great courage, with executioners standing behind them.

The love, respect and reverence of the Companions for the Prophet (upon him blessings and peace) was such that they could hardly describe his physical person:

As Khālid b. Walīd (may Allah be pleased with him) was passing by a Muslim tribe, the sheikh of the tribe asked him to describe the Messenger to him. Khālid replied, "I cannot describe him!"

The chief of the tribe insisted, "Tell me as much as you know!"

Khālid replied:

"I can tell you this much: The status of a messenger is in accordance with the status of the One who sends him. Since the

One Who sent Rasūl Allāh is the Creator of the universe, imagine the status of His Messenger!"

Another great Companion, 'Amr b. al-'Āṣ, responded to the same question in the following way:

"I have never been able to look at the Messenger of Allah (upon him blessings and peace) carefully, because of my veneration for him. Therefore, if I you ask me to describe him, I will not be able to do so."

It is possible to observe the manifestations of the love of the Companions toward the Prophet (upon him blessings and peace) in the way the Companions obeyed his commands and internalized his good character as a role model. The lover follows the beloved to the extent of his love for him. The Messenger of Allah was a mercy to the world, and he looked at creation in its entirety with limitless love and affection.

One of the manifestations of this love on the Companions, who were so attached to him, is narrated by Abū 'Abd al-Rahmān al-Jubulī who said:

During a battle against Byzantium, we were together with Abū Ayyūb al-Ansārī (may Allah be pleased with him) in a ship. Our leader was 'Abd Allāh b. Qays. When the great Companion Abū Ayyūb al-Ansārī came to the man who was in charge of distributing the booty, he saw a crying woman. The woman had been captured during the war. Abū Ayyūb asked why the woman was crying, and they told him, "This woman has a child. They have separated her child from her. That is why she is crying."

Abū Ayyūb al-Ansārī immediately found the child and returned him to his mother. Then the woman stopped crying. The officer who was in charge of the distribution of the booty

Love (mahabbah)

went to the leader of the army, 'Abd Allāh b. Qays, and told him about what Abū Ayyūb had done. When 'Abd Allāh b. Qays asked Abū Ayyūb why he had done this, Abū Ayyūb replied:

I heard from the Messenger of Allah (upon him blessings and peace) the following: "Those who separate a mother from her child, Allah shall separate them, on the Day of Judgment, from all those whom they love." (*Musnad Ahmad*, Tirmidhī).

As made evident by this incident, love for Allah and the Prophet (upon him blessings and peace) requires that all of creation be approached with mercy, affection and love. This is because the greatest fruits of faith are love and mercy.

The following instructive incident further demonstrates the blessings inherent in showing mercy and love to creation, and how such traits lead a human being to the source of faith.

During the time of the Prophet, which is called the Age of Happiness ('*Asr al-Sa'ādah*), there was a person among the Companions called Hakīm b. Hizām. He was a relative of Khadījah, the wife of the Prophet. He was a generous, compassionate, and charitable person. In the pre-Islamic period, commonly called the *Jāhiliyyah* (the age of ignorance prior to Islam), he used to purchase little girls from their fathers who wanted to kill them because they did not want to have a female child. He would save the lives of children and protect them. After embracing Islam, he asked the Prophet (upon him blessings and peace) if the good deeds he had performed prior to becoming a Muslim would help him. The Prophet Muhammad (upon him blessings and peace) indicated in his answer to Hakīm that these good deeds were the reason for his being blessed with conversion to Islam.

If approaching living beings with compassion causes people who are far from true faith to be blessed with the honor of conversion to the true religion, which is the greatest reward, then it is only logical that it will bring even greater rewards to those who are already believers.

True faith is the greatest gift Allah gives to His servants. Our Lord commands that we carefully protect this gift during our lives to the very moment we give up our last breath. The Qur'an states: "O you who believe! Fear Allah as He should be feared, and die not except as Believers." (Āl 'Imrān, 3:102).

The greatest fruit of the blessing of faith is to look at creation with the eyes of the Creator and to approach all creatures with love. This elevates the life of a servant to higher levels and causes him or her to enter a world of forgiveness, mercy and love. One can then spread mercy to all creation. The great friend of Allah, Jalāl al-Dīn Rūmī, illustrates this point well:

A drunken man came to the Sufi lodge while a sermon was being delivered. The disciples in the Sufi path, the dervishes, wanted him to leave, and they insulted him. Rūmī, who approached the drunken man as if he had come to learn about the true faith, said to those who had insulted him: "Although he is the one who has drunk the wine, it seems that you are the ones who are inebriated!"

This story provides a concrete example for how natural feelings of disgust for a sin should not be generalized; in contrast, one should see the sinner as a wounded bird that needs compassionate treatment and accept him into the palace of the heart, where he can be provided with education and guidance. Hoca Ahmed Yesevi illustrated this point beautifully:

Love (mahabbah)

Wherever you see a person with a broken heart, be a cure to him!

If such a oppressed one cannot continue his way, befriend him!

It should not be forgotten that the society of believers with which we are blessed today is a fruit of the Age of Happiness, the time of the Prophet Muhammad (upon him blessings and peace). The great Companions and friends of Allah spent great efforts in transmitting this sacred trust to posterity. They revolved around love for Allah. Thus they became stars in the sky of our faith, teachers in the school of truth, blessings and mercy for our daily lives, the light of our times and the witnesses of Allah the Most Glorious on earth.

The exceptional sacrifices and efforts of the Prophet, his Companions, and the saints and pious servants of Allah in the path of Allah's religion out of divine love must serve as examples for us. To never lose this divine trust that has been entrusted to us, and make efforts to transfer it in its authentic purity and clarity to future generations, are responsibilities with consequences on our eternal happiness in the hereafter. The hearts of believers should continuously experience the joy of faith and divine love at the highest level. This is because real happiness begins after one goes beyond the limited borders of transient love.

The prerequisite for attaining eternal blessing is liberation from the slavery of transient love. Emptying the heart of momentary love is possible only by connecting the ultimate goal of every love to Allah. All good deeds, such as love for homeland or nation, family, children, brotherhood in religion, worship, charity, and good manners lead to divine love and pleasure if they are established on the basis of love for Allah. The deep love of the Companions for Allah and his Messenger (upon him blessings and peace) and the resulting way in which they beheld creation through the sight of their Creator, all exemplify this. They managed to sacrifice their existence as a whole for the sake of their love for Allah. Even the Companions, who did not have a considerable worldly wealth, sacrificed without any hesitation, whatever they earned in their lives, in order not to be separated from Allah and His Messenger and to be with him.

The poet Fuzūlī illustrates in the following example how the heart is the center of love and how one can completely lose oneself in love:

> While Majnūn was wandering around in Leyla's village, foreigners came and asked him where Leyla's home was.
>
> Majnūn replied, "Do not search for her home and tire yourself in vain!"
>
> Then he pointed to his own heart and said, "This is where the home of Leyla is."

We should contemplate the deep meaning and wisdom reflected in this example and question ourselves about the extent to which our hearts are at the point where Allah looks. In other words, to what extent are our hearts full of love for Allah and His Messenger, upon him blessings and peace? Is the joy of faith reflected in our prayers and behavior? Or is love mere rhetoric which does not pass any deeper than our tongues, never to reach our hearts? To what extent is the beating of our hearts, our attitudes and practices in accordance with the Qur'an and the Sunnah? To what extent can we turn transitory worldly blessings into an instrument to gain divine love?

Love (mahabbah)

We need to check our state, as per the principle spelled out by 'Umar (may Allah be pleased with him): "Take account of yourself before you are interrogated in the divine court!" How happy are those who can take an example from the personality and spirituality of Prophet Muhammad (upon him blessings and peace) and thus reach the truth of divine love!

Our Lord! Beautify our hearts with the blessing of faith! Make us among those who see the ugliness of disbelief and disobedience and refrain from them as commanded! Bring us to love those whom You love! Bring us to dislike those whom You dislike! Let us pass away from this world with Your love, with the love of Your Messenger (upon him blessings and peace) and the love of those You love.

Amin!

17.
Interview of Osman Nuri Topbaş on *tasawwuf*

Altinoluk: *In your book "From Faith (Īmān) to Internalization of Faith (Ihsān)," you state that the Sufi path is very important in the life of a Muslim. What are the benefits of the Sufi path in the propagation of Islam, as well as in perfecting and guiding the human soul to the truth? What are the secrets of its success?*

Tasawwuf has a particular method of training people in their practice of Islam. The external aspect of Islam, *sharī'ah*, employs the concepts of reward and punishment in order to lead a human being to a virtuous life. In other words, Paradise and hell are the basic concepts within the *sharī'ah* in shaping the life of a Muslim. On the other hand, *tasawwuf*, which is the internal aspect of Islam, employs love and mercy as its primary methods in addition to the rewards of Paradise and the punishment of hell. Today people are suffering from their sins and straying outside the protective shield of religion. This is a result of their enslavement to their *nafs* (the lower self). Salvation can be offered to sinners through mercy and love. Hence, the methods of *tasawwuf* have gained extra significance since sinners need the soft hand of the Sufi way. It has been observed not only in our country but also in the western world that the Sufi methods have turned many people to Islam. They offer Islam as a life-giving breath to those who have been drowning in the grip of their *nafs* and theories based on logic alone. We should approach sinners not with hatred and revenge, but with hope through mercy and compassion. The sinner is like someone who is drowning in the sea, and it is our duty to extend our hands to that person. Cursing them and scolding them is a deficient method for saving them from their terrible situation.

Human beings, even if they wander far from their real purpose in life, possess great value and honor due to their innate value as human beings. The similarity of a sinner [as mentioned above] is like the sacred Black Stone if it fell to the dust. No Muslim can be indifferent to the sad situation of this precious stone. They would rush to clean it and place it in its proper place, as it came from Paradise and has great value in their eyes. Similarly, when we see a human being we cannot be indifferent to him or her. We should rush to help, whether in material or spiritual terms.

Allah the Almighty informs us that He instilled a spirit from His own presence into human beings when He created them. Therefore each human being possesses divine secrets. No matter how many sins he or she commits, he or she has an innate value that cannot be destroyed by anything.

As Rūmī states, man is similar to pure, clean water through which one can see clearly. However, if this clean water is muddied and mixed with dirt, it does not let us see through it. Similarly, in order to see the divine light one needs to purify this water from the dirt. *Tasawwuf* is a way of purifying a person's soul from the desires of the flesh. Sufis do not exclude anyone from this process of purification, even if that person is immersed in sin. Sufis always offer a chance to anyone who is ready to accept it. There are many examples in the life of the Prophet (upon him blessings and peace) with regard to his mercy for all sorts of sinners.

As an example, the Prophet (upon him blessings and peace) did not exclude Wahshī from his mercy even though he had killed the most beloved uncle of the Prophet, Hamzah (may Allah be pleased with him). The Prophet felt very sad when his uncle was killed by Wahshī at the battle of Uhud. The prophet (upon him blessings and peace) sent him a messenger to accept Islam and to gain eternal salvation. Wahshī in return sent the following message: "O Muhammad! How can you offer me salvation when Allah states in the Qur'an: 'Those who invoke not, with Allah, any other god, nor slay such life as Allah has made sacred, except for just cause, nor commit fornication; and any that does this (not only) meets punishment (but) the penalty on the Day of Judgement will be doubled to him, and he will dwell therein in ignominy.' (*Furqān*, 25:68-69). I have committed all the sins mentioned in this verse, is there any possibility for my salvation?"

To address the misgivings of repentent sinners, Allah Almighty revealed the verse: "Say: 'O My servants who have transgressed against their souls! Despair not of the mercy of Allah: for Allah forgives all sins: for He is oft-forgiving, most merciful." (*Zumar*, 39:53) When Wahshī heard this verse he became very happy and said, "O my Lord! How great is your mercy!" He repented for all his sins with the purpose of never repeating them again, and he accepted Islam along with his friends.

Tasawwuf received its light from such examples from the life of the Prophet (upon him blessings and peace), the recipient of the perfect manifestation of the divine attributes and the one who was favored as the receiver of the divine revelation. According to the Sufis, man possesses a high position on the scale of creation, since he has been created with the potential of becoming the viceregent of Allah on earth. He is like the pupil of the eye in

Interview of Osman Nuri Topbaş on tasawwuf

contrast with the rest of the creation. No sin can eradicate this innate value. *Tasawwuf* views this in a very balanced way. The sinner is tolerated, but this tolerance never extends to the sin itself. We should hate the sin but show mercy to the sinner in order to save him or her from the pit into which he or she has fallen. In so doing, *tasawwuf* provides humanity with the most fruitful method of inviting man to Islam. It is in the nature of man to always yearn for those who extend their arms to them with love and mercy, people such as 'Abd al-Qādir Jīlānī, Yūnus Emre, Bahā' al-Dīn Naqshband, Jalāl al-Dīn Rūmī and other friends of Allah.

> **Altınoluk:** *You have shown us how tasawwuf leads a human being to perfection and cleanses him or her from impurities. In this respect, what place should tasawwuf occupy in the life of a Muslim? Is it possible to lead a pious life without tasawwuf?*

You have asked a very important question. I would like to answer this question by narrating the following story which was told to me by my father Musa Efendi:

We had a neighbor who had converted to Islam (from Christianity). One day I asked him the reason for his acceptance of Islam. He replied:

'I have become Muslim due to the good morality of my neighbor Rabī Molla, who showed good conduct in his trade. He had cows and would earn his livelihood by selling milk. One day he came to our house and gave me a large pot of milk saying, 'This is your milk.' 'You did not owe us any milk,' I answered, thinking that he had made a mistake in delivering the milk to me.

The Secret in the Love for God

This kind and noble person explained why he had brought the milk saying, 'Unfortunately I have seen my cows grazing in your garden when I was unaware. Therefore this milk is yours and I will keep bringing milk to you until the grass is cleaned from its stomach.'

I told him, 'Do not mention it. The grass the cows ate in my garden is nothing valuable and I do not ask anything in return.' He insisted that the milk was my share. He kept bringing milk to my house until the grass was cleaned from the rumen of the cow.

The noble behavior of Rabī Molla moved me very deeply and the veil of heedlessness (*ghafla*) was removed from my eyes. The light of guidance shone in my heart, and I accepted Islam saying to myself: 'The religion of such an upright person is definitely the straight path. No one can doubt the truth of a religion which is professed by such kind, just, and perfect adherents like him.' Hence I pronounced the words of the *shahādah* (the profession of faith).

As this incident and many other countless examples prove, Sufis and their method of perfecting the morality of a believer are important reasons for the spread of Islam. *Tasawwuf* works in both ways: firstly perfecting the morality of the believers, and secondly spreading Islam through the exemplary conduct of Sufis. It shows the merciful face of Islam to the non-Muslims and helps in representing the correct form of Islam.

Islam is law and God-consciousness, *fatwā* and *taqwā*: the legal aspects of Islam, *fatwā*, are the pillars of its edifice, while the Sufi character, *taqwā*, is the complementary part of the building that beautifies and strengthens the main frame. *Tasawwuf* helps Muslims to unite these two aspects of Islam in addition to perfecting their morality. *Tasawwuf* also enables mankind to understand the Qur'an and the universe, helping him to know his place and responsibilities in the universe. *Tasawwuf*, with its principles of love for Allah and knowledge of Allah, is like a vista on *Mi'rāj* – ascension to Allah. In short, the Sufi way is a necessity in training the heart and the soul. Every Muslim needs it.

The question "Can we do without *tasawwuf*?" is like asking if we can we do without hadith, theology, Islamic law, Qur'anic commentary, and the other Islamic sciences. Regarding *tasawwuf* as an unnecessary part of Islam is like regarding such attributes as sincerity, knowledge of Allah, purification of the heart, and the realization of service to Allah as unnecessary! *Tasawwuf* is a term which refers to attaining all these good characteristics. Even those who practice these principles without mentioning the general term that covers them, or who reject the nomenclature of *tasawwuf*, can also be considered to be practicing *tasawwuf*. The name is not important, as long as its principles are put into effect. We can refer to *tasawwuf* as "asceticism" (*zuhd*), "consciousness of Allah" (*taqwā*), or "realization of religion" (*ihsān*), as they all indicate the same reality and serve the same purpose. All these terms denote the practice of the most perfect master and teacher of humanity, the Prophet Muhammad (upon him blessings and peace) and the companions whom he himself trained.

The heart also needs training in order to attain peace and tranquility. Even the Prophet (upon him blessings and peace) who was blessed with reception of the divine revelation, had special training before he attained prophethood. He used to go to the cave of Hira and spend his time in worship and contemplation. This special dedication of time to worship is called in Arabic *i'tikāf*. The Prophet (upon him blessings and peace) continued this practice after he became a Prophet, and spent the last ten days of the month of Ramadan in the mosque dedicating all his time to worship. Similarly, the Prophet Moses spent forty days in worship and mortification of the flesh before he was blessed with being able to speak with Allah on the mountain of Sinai. The Prophet Joseph spent twelve years in prison before he became the ruler of Egypt. He went trough all sorts of difficulties and perfected his personality as through the worship of Allah. In this way, his heart was cleansed from trust in transient beings and was eventually dedicated to Allah alone.

Before the *Mi'rāj* (ascension), the Prophet Muhammad (upon him blessings and peace) grasped the meaning of the chapter of *inshirāh* (expanding). His spiritual heart was opened and cleansed. Allah the Almighty filled his heart with knowledge and divine light. In this way he was prepared to see the extraordinary things his voyage to Allah showed him. He was cleansed from the material world and was prepared for the spiritual world.

If even the prophets of Allah underwent spiritual training and purification of the heart, how can ordinary people like ourselves do without this process? Even a hair that remains polluted with worldly concerns cannot approach the divine light of the spiritual world. A nose blocked with dirt cannot smell the aroma of flowers and roses. When the window is steamed up we cannot see through it clearly. A small clod of dirt can pollute a whole pot of pure water; similarly, spiritual dirt blocks the heart from the reception of divine illumination and spiritual blessing.

In order to emphasise the significance of a purified heart from all sorts of worldly diseases, Allah the Almighty states in the Qur'an: "The day whereon neither wealth nor sons will avail, but only he (will prosper) that brings to Allah a sound heart!" (*Shu'arā'*, 26:88-89)

Interview of Osman Nuri Topbaş on tasawwuf

One can attain a heart which is sound and free from all sorts of evil thoughts only through spiritual training. Before such training, the heart is like a piece of raw iron. First it should be heated with fire and cleansed of all dirt. Then it should be hammered and molded into the shape intended. Once the heart is perfected through spiritual training, it can see and understand what the physical eyes cannot see and the mind cannot understand. [As mentioned before,] Rūmī describes his own state before spiritual wayfaring as being unripe, even though he occupied a high post in a Seljuk *madrasa*. However, when the secrets of the book of the universe were opened to him through spiritual training, he described his new state saying, "I was cooked."

The companions of the Prophet (upon him blessings and peace) constitute the highest examples of this spiritual perfection. Before Islam came, some of them had such cold hearts that they used to bury their daughters alive. However, after accepting Islam they became monuments of mercy and soft-heartedness.

In short, we could practice Islam without *tasawwuf*, but then we would never reach our perfection. When Sufi methods are excluded from the practice of Islam, none can reach the level of Islamic practice known as *ihsān* (i.e. to practice Islam as if seeing Allah).

> **Altınoluk:** *What else would you advise the readers of Altınoluk? Who are your spiritual friends on the Sufi path? We are sure that they will be awaiting the English version of your book "From Faith (Īmān) to Internalisation of Faith (Ihsān)," in which you have given a detailed explanation of tasawwuf.*

In addition to what I have said so far, let me add some advice which the Sufi sheikhs have emphasised. *Tasawwuf* is the method of moral training taken from the life and teaching of the Messenger of Allah (upon him blessings and peace). It consists of turning one's face with love and respect towards Allah and His Messenger. Those friends of Allah who have placed Allah and His Messenger at the center of their hearts as the sole objects of love, have become the friends of all humanity. To keep friendship with the pious Muslims and take part in their *suhbah*s purifies one's morality from evil. Those who have a high level of spiritual energy spread their energy to others. Since they have purified their own souls from the vices of the *nafs*, they can inculcate the same state of spiritual purity to those around them. Being around such people makes one beneficial to the community in all aspects of life.

Through love, *tasawwuf* establishes spiritual bonds between the desciple (*murīd*) and his master (*shaykh*). Once the *murīd* loves and respects the *shaykh*, the actions of the *shaykh* are imitated from all perspectives, and the morality of the *murīd* is perfected. Therefore, as Muslims we should use the method of love more often than other methods. The basis of Islamic morality is to worship Allah with sincerity and love. The proof of love and sincerity is to serve Allah and His creation. Through love, difficult jobs are fulfilled with ease and contentment. The greatness of service is judged by the sacrifice taken in its fulfillment. Sincere service is the indication of one's spiritual perfection. The hearts of such people are the loci of the manifestations (*tajalliyāt*) of Allah.

The closer one gets to Allah, the more his or her heart becomes receptive to spiritual realities. On the other hand, the more one is engulfed in his or her *nafs* (lower self), the more he or she loses his or her humanity.

Interview of Osman Nuri Topbaş on tasawwuf

Allah has the names *Jamīl* (the Beautiful) and *Jalīl* (the Majestic). However, his names *Rahmān* (the Compassionate) and *Rahīm* (the Merciful) are mentioned in the Qur'an more than any other of His names. Therefore, in the imitation of his or her Lord, a Muslim should make mercy and compassion his or her second nature. The causes of injustice in the world are the result of a lack of mercy and love. Those who cannot love can easily become despots and tyrants. They use fear and hate in order to control others, remaining heedless of the fact that there is no heart that cannot be captured by love. For the sun to refuse to give light and heat is impossible; similarly, it is impossible for righteous souls not to love and show mercy to other creatures.

Hallāj who has an exclusive place in the hearts of the divine lovers prayed for those who had stoned him to death saying, "O my Lord please forgive those who have stoned me to death before You forgive me!"

If we would like to know our spiritual state, we should continuously analyze our actions and feelings. In particular, the baseless claims of our *nafs* should be kept under control. Otherwise we could fall into the state of Iblīs, who lost divine favor due to his haughtiness and vanity. He was the teacher of the angels in Paradise, but he could not control his emotions and desires. He felt superior to human beings and was cursed due to his pride.

Rūmī compares the vices of human nature to thorns on a rose bush. He advises us to make our nature like that of the sweet rose, not that of thorns. In the garden of the world the thorns harm us, but we should not let our soul become like them. Rather, we should strive to convert the wild soil into a rose garden.

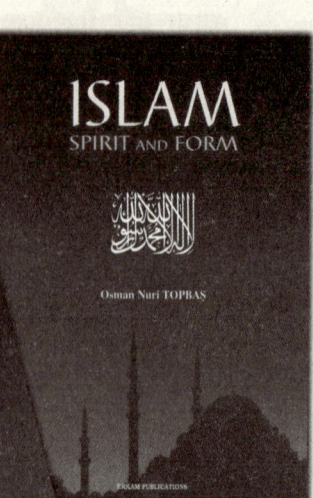

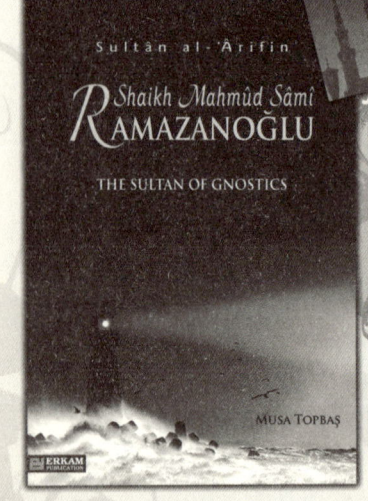

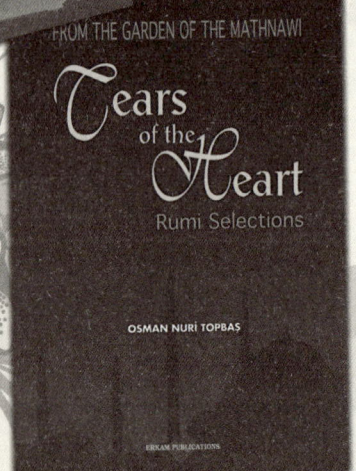

www.islamicpublishing.net